CHASING THE MONSTER IDEA

THE MARKETER'S ALMANAC FOR PREDICTING IDEA EPICNESS

STEFAN MUMAW

WILEY

John Wiley & Sons, Inc.

Published by John Wiley & Sons, Inc., Hoboken, New Jersey.
Published simultaneously in Canada.

Book design by Stefan Mumaw
Cover illustration by Von Glitschka

For general information on our other products and services or for technical support, please contact our Customer Care Department within the United States at (800) 762-2974, outside the United States at (317) 572-3993 or fax (317) 572-4002.

Wiley also publishes its books in a variety of electronic formats. Some content that appears in print may not be available in electronic books. For more information about Wiley products, visit our web site at www.wiley.com.

ISBN 978-0-470-91585-1 (cloth)
ISBN 978-1-118-06071-1 (ebk)
ISBN 978-1-118-04953-2 (ebk)
ISBN 978-1-118-06070-4 (ebk)

Printed in the United States of America

10 9 8 7 6 5 4 3 2 1

Monster idea makers are rare. They lurk in the shadows of mediocrity waiting to break the darkness with deviant concepts and risky ideas. They're energizing and inspiring, and over the course of my life, they've helped form my philosophy on creativity and ideation and encouraged me to continue looking under the bed for what may be waiting.

This book of monsters is dedicated to them: Denise Weyhrich, Eric Chimenti, Wendy Lee Oldfield, Trevor Gerhard, Chris Brown, and Mike Kelly.

Thanks for the scares.

Contents

Rule of The Proverbial Thumb

Throughout the book, I reference a variety of commercial TV spots and videos as we examine monster and not so monster campaigns. Instead of including flip-book-style drawings in the corners of each chapter, I put links to the spots on the Super Uber Official "Chasing The Monster Idea" Web site. Any time you see the above filmreel icon appear, it will be accompanied by a slash-name denoting where you can see that spot.

For instance, if you ran across this callout within the pages of a chapter:

 /RappersDelight

You would be ultra-keen to type in:

www.ChasingTheMonsterIdea.com/RappersDelight

Where, of course, you'd be redirected to video of horrifying marketing relevance.

Carry on.

"I have an idea."

That's what Alex said to me just before he laid out his master plan for community domination. Alex and I met just after college when he started looking for a local design firm to develop the logo for his one-man pest control company. He came from a long line of exterminators, which I always thought was a killer thing to say at parties. (Pun intended. Laugh, dammit!) Alex was completely consumed with a passion to make it on his own, he wanted nothing more than to succeed without his parent's help and out from under his parent's name. I applauded his initiative and was drawn to his passion. I've always been drawn to people who have a passion for whatever. You could have a deep-rooted passion for human taxidermy and I'd probably still be drawn to you. (That was an example, not an invitation. No, seriously.)

Alex's logo was one of the first I designed professionally, and I was quite proud of it. I entered it in every design contest imaginable thinking this was going to be the project that put me on the map. Looking back now, the mark is so decisively atrocious, I wouldn't dare show it to anyone I liked. Even if I didn't like you, I'd probably still shield you from the horror (and as evidenced by it's absence from this page, consider yourself mercifully saved). Alex, however, loved it and we developed a friendship around the work. We've grown apart over the years, and I'd like to think it had nothing to do with my impassioned encouragement to put his time, money, and reputation behind what was quite possibly:

the worst idea

Alex and I had been throwing around ideas to generate some buzz for his new company (again, pun intended. Get used to it. As a matter of fact, if I fail to mention that a pun was intended, and you find it even remotely chuckle worthy, go ahead and assume it was intentional. Just covering my bases.). Like everyone I've ever done business with, he didn't have much money to spend but was convinced that the creativity of two bright guys like us would generate ideas previously unknown to human kind. Of course, I was hesitant to disagree. After all, I just graduated with a degree in graphic design for Pete's sake. I wasn't just some poor, inexperienced schmuck off the street, I was educated . . . and in design nonetheless! This was going to be One Show worthy, I could feel it in my black turtleneck.

We spent a couple nights throwing around ideas, going back and forth about cost and effectiveness. He was fond of saying "not enough bang for the buck, brah." I was fond of envisioning creative ways of wrapping his tongue around his melon after hearing it the first 16 times, but in most cases, he was right and the constant rejection was pushing us to think larger. And that's when he said it.

I so wish he never said it, because I know I would never have suggested it. I would be forced to tell you a completely different tale of epic, humiliating failure to make my point. More important, *someone else's* epic, humiliating failure. But he said it, and I grabbed it like he just suggested the cure for male pattern baldness.

man has ever thunk.

"I read somewhere that Coke pays for the menu boards at a lot of the fast-food restaurants that sell Coke so they can control the Coke message and imagery on the board. The fast-food joint gets the value of free menu boards and Coke gets to make sure they are positioned right. That's a pretty good idea. We should do the same thing. My buddy, Rob, works at his dad's pizza joint. What if we offered to pay for all their pizza boxes if they'd let us put our ad on the box? That way, every person in the neighborhood that orders their pizza gets our ad. We get ad space and distribution for the cost of a few boxes!"

I could hardly contain myself. I was both excited and angry. Excited by the possibilities but angry that exterminator boy came up with that idea and not me, the trained professional. Bastard! I wouldn't let him out-idea me. I had to take it to the next level:

"That's a great idea! But why stop there? One pizza shop covers too small an area, let's go to every mom-and-pop pizza shop in the area and offer the same thing! And not just pizza shops, but Chinese take-outs, frozen yogurt shops, hole-in-the-wall burger joints, let's hit them all!"

That, in and of itself, was actually a decent idea. It created an experience, it would confront unexpectedly and it was targeted. The only thing left to do was to come up with the message. We couldn't just put his logo and phone number on the packages, regardless of how life-changing the experience of seeing the logo would surely be. I thought it would take a little more than that, even if it was only slightly more (insert wry, arrogant smile here). We needed to do something so memorable, so creative that people would naturally say, "What an amazing idea, I simply must know who came up with it. Shortly after having my mansion bug-bombed, I need to talk with the savant that came up with that idea. If he can do it for the exterminator, he can do it for my Fortune 100 company." Or something like that. And the idea I had in my head would do all that and more. It was a big idea. BIG. I'd never seen it done, so it had to be big. That's the sign of a great idea, right? That I've never seen it done. I was, after all, a design major. I'd seen waaaaaay more than Alex; he would have to listen to me.

"Alex, here's what I think will make a HUGE impact for you. It's revolutionary, it's perfect. Before I tell you, I have to ask what your business model is prepared to hold right now, in terms of volume. Will you have the infrastructure to deal with hundreds of calls almost instantly? I don't want to overload you if you're not ready yet. Okay, here's what we do. Instead of just a logo and phone number on the boxes, we print an image of a bug at the bottom of each container, along with the headline 'Bugs can hide anywhere, be prepared' with your logo and phone number! On each box, we could even customize the message to go with the food type, like 'Little known fact: roaches prefer teriyaki sauce to sweet-and-sour' or something witty like that. It's brilliant! Folks will think you are the coolest exterminator in town! And if it's okay with you, I'd like to offer doing it for free if you'll let me put my name and number down as the creative genius behind the ad. Whatcha think?!"

From the moment I said ". . . bug at the bottom," Alex had a strange smile on his face. It was the type of expression that I have grown to know as the "UM" face because it's usually followed by a "Ya, umm, Stef . . . I don't know about that" type of response. This was no different. Alex had reservations. Part of me was joyful of his doubts, as I had taken my rightful throne back as the creative genius of the pair, but part of me knew I was going to have to convince him that while I knew it sounded a little risky (not to me, to me it was pure, unadulterated genius), I had bucketsful of experience in stuff like this, and it was going to generate more business than he could possibly handle. I spread it on thick with questions like "do you have contacts for other exterminators you could throw the overflow work to until you ramp up?" and quips about him "killing it." He finally gave in, and I went home to clear space over my TV for the giant gold pencils.

Our agreement was easy: I did the work for free, and he paid for the boxes and the printing. I even went with him over a few weekends to secure our restaurant participants. The reception to the idea of providing free boxes was met with an overwhelming acceptance. We were in business.

The day was finally here: delivery day. We had a garage full of boxes, cartons, cups and containers, each adorned with a different bug and a different headline. I decided not to wait for Alex; I went and delivered each of the packages to the restaurants personally. No one opened the packages, they just accepted them and I was told they'd put them into play as soon as that night. I started clearing my calendar for the inevitable flood of business that was surely coming my way. I told Alex to do the same.

The next week and a half was a bit of a blur, thinking back now. I remember getting my first package-related call the next day, from

an ice cream shop owner that evidently didn't find the creativity as ingenious as I did. No matter, there's always going to be naysayers who don't like a creative approach. What do they know, anyway? But after eight solid days of phone calls that ranged from crank-call-obscene to scathing and profanity-laden, I began to reevaluate my assumptions. Alex did, too. He was inundated with store owners, managers, and end-customers contacting him to inform him of what they believed was the most disgusting, distasteful ad they had ever seen and even if their wallpapers were physically lifting off the walls and repositioning themselves with pests, they would rather bathe in Raid than employ his services.

Um, oops.

What could possibly have gone wrong? That idea was destined for greatness, right? Um, wrong. When I developed that idea, I was completely engrossed with its possibilities. My design professor had always told me that a great idea dislodges people. This idea dislodged people, certainly. But what was missing was a host of other characteristics that play just as important a role to the success of the idea as alarm does.

When you read the story, and you came to the part where I described the idea in detail, you most certainly had no problem deciding that this idea was doomed for a fiery death, did you? (If you didn't, please return to the bookstore and purchase another nine copies of this book, just in case you lose this one.) Why was it, then, that a professional creative destined for glory and greatness such as myself couldn't see what a terrible, appalling idea it was at the time? I mean, don't we all believe we have the ability to differentiate a good idea from a bad idea? Internet access on a plane = good, pay toilets on a plane = bad. There are few people, if any, that would openly admit they have difficulty determining a good idea from a bad one. Unfortunately, though, it's not always a black-and-white matter. There have been plenty of ideas I thought would fail that succeeded, and plenty I thought would succeed that failed miserably (one comes to mind). Sometimes, the predictive waters of an idea's success is murky. Other times, it's clear to see. Let's see how you do with this one: In 2000, Nike wanted to reinforce the versatility of their new Nike Air Cross Trainer II shoe while increasing quality branding time with their audience. Nike has always been athlete-centric, so they wanted the audience to experience this athlete-centric brand message of the athletic-wear superpower in a completely different way. What if the viewer wasn't just watching a commercial, but was *in* the commercial, controlling it in some way?

The resulting campaign was called "Whatever" and it featured famous Nike athletes engaged in their sport. Instead of watching the action passively, the spot put the viewer right in the commercial and asked them what they'd do. The first spot featured then red-hot Olympian Marion Jones and dropped the viewer into an immediate first-person challenge. The spots faded to black before the climax of the story, leading the viewer to the Web site to choose how it would end from seven different endings. Armed with more time with the viewer, the endings could be as long and entertaining as the creators wanted. /Jones

For example, the first spot featuring Jones begins with the premise "You're racing Marion Jones. The fastest woman in the world. What do you do?" Jones then challenges the viewer to a race through the streets of Santa Monica, California. She races down the world-famous promenade, dodging street performers and meandering through groups of tourists. The viewer, on the other hand, chases behind her and eventually slams into a chain saw juggler, who tosses the chain saws into the air on contact. As the chain saws fall back to the ground, the screen goes black and says "Continued at whatever.nike.com." The Web site concludes the story with seven possible endings, like letting the chain saws fall and chasing Jones into a garage, where a boxing trainer fits you both for boxing gloves and you duke it out (eventually losing your teeth when Jones pops you silly) or you end up on the back of a two-person bike pedaling down the beach-front walkway, Jones in the front, while you constantly reach out to try and grab Jones but are always inches away. The spot always ends with Jones getting the better of you because she is a Nike athlete (plus, she's way faster than you anyway). Entertaining and dripping with brand character, the endings almost forced you to watch them all to see what could happen.

So, good idea or bad idea? You had me worried there, you took a second to respond. Of course it's a good idea! The campaign was an instant hit, drawing media attention to the point that TV stations were afraid to run the spots. They felt that people would leave the TV and go straight to the Web to finish the story. The Nike Air Cross Trainer II almost immediately shot to number one in Nike sales and was outselling the nearest competitor 10-to-1. All in all, a monster idea.

Now compare the Nike "Whatever" idea with my cockroach idea. Why was the Nike "Whatever" idea a huge success and easily defined as a good idea while my exterminator campaign went down in flames? There are obvious assumptions we make: Nike authentically tapped the emotion and curiosity of their well-defined audience. The cockroach disaster is a self-serving advertisement meant to line the pockets of commercially minded entrepreneurs. All valid points, yes (although I feel even more shallow than I did prior to that sentence). But strip away the purpose of the idea and get down to the quality of the idea itself and you'll discover they're not that different after all.

Both start with a problem: In one instance, there's a desire to expand a brand message and in turn sell more shoes, and in the other, there's a desire to see a community informed of a new, available resource in a cost-effective way. The degree of problem is certainly inequitable, but there is still a problem to be solved in both cases.

Both benefit from nontraditional methods to solve the problem: In one instance, the mixture of TV and the Internet were rare, especially when story and video were part of the equation and in the other, traditional cost-effective advertising methods like flyers or direct mail goes relatively unnoticed.

Both were dislodging in concept: In one instance, the cliffhanger endings created an immediate desire to see completion and do so in an entertaining way and in the other, the unexpected placement of messaging was sure to be noticed and absorbed.

In those terms, both ideas carry similar attributes. So why is the Nike "Whatever" idea so much more successful, both in perception and in reality, then the cockroach campaign idea? The answer lies in the totality of their characteristics. They share the above traits, but those traits don't define the success or failure of an idea by themselves. And they certainly don't predict the probability, at an idea's inception, that the idea has the chance to go from good to great or great to monster.

A good idea is an idea that simply solves a problem. I'm hungry and my wife suggests hitting Chipotle for dinner. That's a good idea. I'm hungry and my wife suggests robbing Chipotle for dinner. That's a bad idea.

A great idea is an idea that solves a problem creatively. I'm hungry and my wife suggests grilling steaks at home and watching the game. That's a great idea. I'm hungry and my wife suggests grilling eggplant and watching *Steel Magnolias*. That's a terrible idea.

But a monster idea is one that is more than good, it transcends the boundaries of the problem and solves it with such simplicity and fullness, it almost tells itself. The monster idea is fluidly passed from person to person, barely requiring any force beyond initiation. It swells and grows on its own, carried by an ever-expanding group of evangelists that latch on to its side like remoras alongside sharks, taking it wherever the idea wishes to go. Monster ideas manifest themselves in many ways, we've seen them in traditional creative circles like advertising and design to more organic entities like government and social culture. Any place a problem exists, examples of monster ideas can be found. The question is:

How do we recognize an idea's potential to be monster?

As per our previous example, it's not difficult to see monster ideas in hindsight, but it's exponentially harder to predict if an idea has monster idea potential. The originator of the idea is quite possibly the worst soothsayer of an idea's potential, as was so painfully proven by The Great Cockroach Debacle. As idea originators, we are all incredibly passionate about our ideas, often filling in the holes of an idea's possibility with rose-colored spackle. It's not uncommon for an originator to respond to the question "Well, what about this obstacle?" with "Oh, I'm sure it'll be just fine!"

<Painful Example Sidenote>

Alex: *"Um, Stef, ya . . . it sounds like a good idea and all, but what about the people that get to the bottom of their chicken fried rice and see the june bug but not the payoff headline? When they gag and hurl soy sauce on the kitchen floor only to discover it's an ad for a pest control company, don't you think they're gonna be mad?"*

Stefan: *"Oh, I'm sure it'll be just fine!"*

</End Painful Example Sidenote>

Friends and family fare only slightly better at influencing the originator of the idea's monster, or lack of monster, potential because as necessary as passion is to the growth and development of an idea, passion also clouds judgment. It takes a mature originator to be swayed from their belief, and rightfully so. Some of the most monster of ideas came from a complete ignorance of surrounding opinion. But I would contend that there have been a far greater number of right idea critics than wrong idea critics.

How many times has a friend or family member come to you with an idea that is clear (in your mind) to be an absolutely horrendous idea with a 1.67 percent chance of succeeding? I bet it happens far more than a friend or family member coming to you with a clearly monster idea. Why can we see the writing on the wall so clearly for them but so turbidly for us? Because the originator is always the most passionate and therefore the most clouded.

What we need is an objective gauge against which to judge our ideas. In reality, the perfect solution would be to find the Oracle from the *Matrix* movies and rent her out to ideators. We could simply ask her if our idea will be a monster idea. The problem is she'd tell us exactly what we needed to hear. Plus, it would be so cryptic a response we'd have no idea one way or the other anyway. Okay, example of a bad idea.

No, what we need is a barometer for ideas, something that we can measure the qualities and characteristics of our ideas against to help predict if the idea is as undeniably strong as we think it is. While there is no tried-and-true method to determine if our ideas will be as big as we think they could be, it would be incredibly helpful to have something to measure our ideas against, some form of comparison to make. Since we often view uniqueness as a quality of a big idea, it's always been difficult to compare ideas, as few are exactly alike. As soon as we see another idea that is similar to ours, we immediately feel our idea now lacks the potential to be monstrous, as we've lost the one true measure of greatness: novelty (not entirely true, but certainly helpful). What we need is a way to dissect other ideas surgically to diagnose what *made* them big, what foundational characteristic led to their overwhelming success. We need a measuring stick.

A measuring stick is, as you would suspect, a stick used to measure the length of something in comparison. It doesn't have any markings or divisions on it, it simply is a reference tool. It can be used to measure anything as it has no defined measurement assigned to it.

Taking the literal definition out of it for now, we have seen many things in our cultural history become their own measuring sticks on which future iterations are judged. It's not uncommon for monster ideas to create new measuring sticks for an industry or category. In 1954, a man by the name of Ray Kroc was selling milkshake machines to restaurants and stumbled across a hamburger joint that had an unusually efficient production line style of food preparation. Recognizing the monster idea potential, he purchased the franchise rights from the owners and eventually bought out the remaining partners to own outright what would become the measuring stick for a new quickly prepared restaurant category called "fast food": McDonald's.

Often, measuring sticks in product categories are recreated with the introduction of new technology or product offerings, effectively lengthening the measuring stick and creating new subcategories through innovation. In 2005, Apple and Motorola got together to release the first mobile phone that included support for iTunes, Apple's flagship music purchasing and management software. Apple CEO Steve Jobs was unhappy with the limitations of sharing technology development with Motorola, so he set out to see his monster idea developed internally. In 2007, the current measuring stick for a new category of mobile phones called "smartphones" arrived in the Apple iPhone. It wasn't the first smartphone on the market, but its monster ideas made it the measuring stick upon which all future smartphones are judged. Of course, there will inevitably be a new measuring stick developed in the future, as the circulation of technology never ceases.

Almost every category or industry has a measuring stick example, including subcategories within our focus: advertising and marketing. An ad agency out of Miami had a desire to generate a Web site that would be passed around from person to person through e-mail, chat, and natural conversation that could work as a traffic leader to communicate their client's brand character. Their monster idea was to dress a guy up in a chicken suit, put him on camera and allow people to control his movements through a text field input on the site. The goal was to promote their fast-food client's new chicken menu and their solution, Subservient Chicken, became the measuring stick to a new avenue of digital conversation: viral communication.

In each of these cases, the measuring stick for the industry or category was created by a monster idea but there were certainly opportunities in each case to see or develop less than a monster idea. Ray Kroc could have seen the McDonald brothers' operation and thought, "The assembly line metaphor is a good idea, I'm going to apply that to how I sell milkshake machines" (good idea) or "The assembly line metaphor is a great idea, I'm going to buy their restaurant from them" (great idea) but he didn't. He saw the potential to create multiple franchises using this business practice and McDonald's, the monster idea, was born.

How did Ray Kroc see the monster idea potential in one restaurant's process? How did Steve Jobs shake off the epic failure of the Newton MessagePad, Apple's first touch screen PDA, and turn that technology into the current standard in mobile communication? How did Crispin Porter + Bogusky know that people would frequently and freely pass along their chicken-dancing Web site in such volume? Simply put, there was a universal understanding that each idea met certain idea characteristics that gave some insight into the idea's potential to go from good to great to monster.

Some people have an innate ability to see things through monster idea glasses. They can instantly process an idea's potential and be able to measure whether the idea has a chance at monsterdom. These people, in one way or another, are processing the characteristics of the idea to determine its potential awesomeness, characteristics that we can use to predict an idea's chance at monsterdom, too. All we have to do is interrogate the idea and see how it responds.

This is the hardest part for idea originators, by the way. Removing ourselves from the idea and interrogating it objectively is painful. The idea is our baby, we carried it, bore it, nurtured it, and fed it. Now, we are asking ourselves to sit it in a chair in a dark room, shine a bright light on it and ask it questions until it breaks. ("Where were you on the night of the 15th?!" "I was in your sketchbook! You were there! Why are you doing this to me?!")

While interrogating our ideas sounds heartwrenching, it's necessary to determine if our ideas have the chance to go monster like we think they do. Until we break down and ask the right questions of our ideas, their chance of success is a guess at best. But what questions to ask?

In their book *Made to Stick*, Chip and Dan Heath report upon a pattern they found in their research of why certain ideas stick and others don't. Their research, through interviews with dozens of storytellers, psychologists, and political scientists, revealed that sticky ideas all shared common traits, but no distinct formula exists. Ideas that stick tend to be simple, unexpected, clear, credible, emotional, and story driven. They don't have to be all of these to stick, but almost all ideas that tend to stick fall into at least one of these camps.

By contrast, we're not going to explore what characteristics make any idea stick but rather what characteristics make marketing and advertising ideas grow. In the creative industry, we generate an innumerable amount of ideas every day; some bad, some good, some great, and once in a blue moon (or insert the oddly colored celestial body of your choice) a monster idea that garners a reaction far greater than we were expecting. While we knew it was a great idea, we didn't know how great until it was released into the wild and started scaring unsuspecting campers. It's the hope of every marketer: to create something that not only does what it was designed to do (that is, sell more product or raise more awareness), but does so with such force and with such verve that the audience doesn't just remember it, or even that they respond positively to it, but they evangelize for it. When the audience becomes the messenger of an idea, gather the mob and sharpen the pitchforks . . . your idea's gone monster.

/Voyeur

When we're focusing our attention on marketing or advertising ideas, specifically the potential for the ideas we think are big ideas to be, in fact, monstrous, we have a slightly different measuring stick. For instance, BBDO's award-winning "Voyeur" campaign for HBO, which involved a cross-section projection onto a large New York City apartment building where passersby could tune in to hear the activities occurring within different apartments, wasn't necessarily simple but it did pass into monsterdom in successful buzz for both HBO and BBDO because the creators were able to interrogate the idea strategically and determine it had the chops. In the end, it wasn't simplicity that captivated the concept's creators, it was a lethal combination of monster idea characteristics that made the concept's savage success clearer to predict.

So what do we ask of our ideas to find out if they're as big as we think they are or if they're really The Great Cockroach Debacle in sheep's clothing? (I wish that upon no one. Except the Greek joint owner who swore at me violently in what I'm assuming is Greek. It was all Greek to me.) When we break down our ideas, there are six-plus-one core questions we need to ask to determine monstrous potential. Notice I didn't say there were seven core questions, I said there were six-plus-one. There are six core questions we need to ask of our idea and one general feeling we need to search for within ourselves to begin to predict an idea's potential for epicness. The common thread between most monster ideas can be found in a positive response to all or most of these questions. The more positive the response, the better the chance of a monsterlicious result.

For instance, let's take an example of a wildly successful monster idea, one that contains a serving of all six monster idea characteristics, and we'll use it as a measuring stick for our own idea. In each chapter, as we discuss the monster characteristic, we'll come back to this example and touch on how that characteristic played a role in this idea's monsterdom:

In 2008, Microsoft turned to ad agency McCann Worldgroup SF to help them plan the launch of the Xbox 360 Halo 3 video game. Halo 2 was one of the most successful game launches in the history of the industry, and Microsoft wanted to top the success with the new title. McCann Worldgroup SF spent months with the game, its creators, writers, and with fans and enthusiasts. Their monster idea: **Believe.**

McCann Worldgroup SF created a campaign that centered around the main character in the game, Master Chief, and one mythical battle. They created TV and online video documentaries using real-life characters in the future, reliving Master Chief's performance in the battle as if they were really there. Set in the future, they created the fictional Museum of Humanity that documented the battle, the weapons, and the enemy. Real-life former "soldiers" even walked the documentary film crew through the fictional battle at fictional locations where Master Chief's heroics saved the platoon . . . and the war.

The campaign was a monster success. Halo 3 made $170 million on the first day of release and has sold 8.1 million units worldwide. Throughout our exploration, we'll take a look back at this monster idea and begin to dissect the campaign to identify what characteristics played a role in the idea turning monster in hopes of illustrating how these same characteristics can become the harbinger of monstrous things to come within our own ideas.

Along with this look back, each chapter will conclude with a characteristic tear page that summarizes the take-aways from that chapter. Literally tear the page away as a reminder of the important points surrounding that characteristic. Tape it to your work area next to a picture of me. Or just the tear sheet, whatever floats your boat.

So let's get to the monster idea characteristics already, GAWSH! Ask your idea these questions, and let the games begin.

/Believe

You don't know how you got there, but there you are, on a grassy hill overlooking a dark but strangely active valley. The wind gently carries the distinct fragrance of scorched earth past you while a constant hum rises to the sky. You're also on a horse, which is equally odd because you haven't the slightest idea what to do should the horse decide to move (screaming like a little girl while you bear hug your steed's neck seems inappropriate considering the apparent rank you've inherited as evidenced by your lofty perch). As you look down into the valley, all five of your senses take in the epic scene simultaneously: a battle. But this battle seems peculiar to you. While there are clearly opposing forces engaged in combat, the weapons seem to be more appropriate to an office insurrection than a battleground. The combatants are wielding newspapers and magazines, waving car stereos and handheld mobile devices. Dear god, they are hurling Internets at each other, lobbing popular sitcoms and attacking with loaded tablet PCs. The ammunition? Bullet . . . points. At least from one side. The bullet points seem to be . . . yes, they're features and benefits of products and services. One guy just flung a price violator at another guy and hit him with the "only" hanging off the end. Horrific.

On the other side, it looks like they're assaulting with something quite different. They're arming themselves with laughter, some dude over there is crying, and they're firing a steady barrage of relatability and humanity. Armed with a lethal mix of anxiety and amusement, this side isn't bludgeoning the other but rather . . . yes . . . they're planting seeds of appeal all over the battlefield! No way this works, right? No way they . . . HOLY CRAP! It worked! The sides are lowering their flat-screen TVs and putting away their

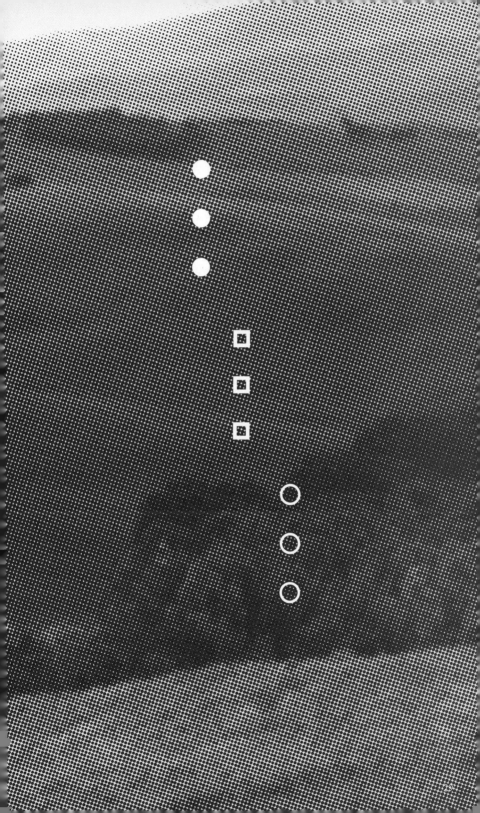

direct-mail postcards, now walking hand in hand toward a light on the far hill. What is that light, where is it coming from? Oh, it's a Walmart. Got it.

What you've just hallucinated is either the result of far too many umbrella drinks or the marketing war that's been waging for years, a war between purchase drivers. On one side are the rational purchase drivers we all use to base our purchase behavior. On the other, the emotional purchase drivers that lead us to become brand loyalists over time. This battle surfaces each and every time we choose to communicate a message to our audience. The question for marketers becomes:

"What message will compel them to buy more (insert your product here) or give more (insert your charitable deliverable here) or order more (insert your undisclosed, craft-paper-wrapped Internet order here)?"

The answer, all too often, is "once they understand what a great product or service this is, and at such an acceptable cost, they'll naturally come in droves flinging their commerce at us repeatedly!" So the communication to this audience drips with product features, service benefits, price advantages, and a host of other rational purchase drivers intent on convincing the audience that the product or service in question is better, faster, cheaper than the competition. The most difficult aspect of this argument is that it's not wrong, it's just not how we, as consumers, exclusively choose what and when to buy.

The argument breaks down on two levels. First, the product is only better, faster, cheaper until someone else comes along and offers something better, faster, and cheaper. Then, we have to add "used to be" to our list of features or change the product deliverables and price to again become better, faster, cheaper (we internally call this the "er" mentality. Bett-er, fast-er, cheap-er. It's a never-ending cycle that usually ends in unworkable profit margins and reactive business practices. Run from the "er" mentality. Run fast . . . er). Second, the argument doesn't take into account what makes a product or service truly great in the eyes of the consumer. It's not always the features, benefits, and price that lure us to consume, although those are certainly factors. Each of us assigns something vital to every purchase decision we make, and it's this single characteristic that defines what and when we buy:

value.

Value is an intimate measure, it's different for each person. Individually, value is different in each buying situation. Value is defined to us by a number of factors on both sides of the rational/emotional line and those factors change depending on what and when we are buying. Each time we choose to buy, we weigh five value categories: Product, Price, Equity, Experience, and Convenience. Carrying around a basic understanding of these categories and the role they play in the purchase process helps us understand what messages will resonate with our audiences most and can help us predict whether the idea we have has the chance to go monster or scatter and cower when the lights come on.

Product is the value we place on the features and benefits of what we are buying. How good is this product? How does it compare to similar products? What will I be able to do with this product that (a) I can't do now, and (b) I can't do with a competitive product?

Price is both the absolute cost of the product (how much in actual dollars does this product cost) and the relative cost of the product (how much does this product cost versus how much I have versus how much a competitive product with greater or lesser features might cost). Yes, that hurt my head, too. Think of it as more cost than price. What will this product cost me and am I willing to pay for what the product delivers?

Equity is the brand promise delivered over time that you get from a product. How much do I trust this company to deliver on the promises of this product? Will it live up to my expectations? Will I regret this purchase because the product is less than what the company claimed it to be? What is my personal opinion of the company or product's reputation?

Experience is how you have interacted with a brand and the feeling you received from the interaction. Does the company behind this product value my time and my patronage enough to ensure I always have a positive experience with their brand? Do they entertain me? Do they comfort me? Have past experiences been equally as positive?

Convenience is the value of the energy we need to exert to acquire the product. How much effort does it take to get this product? Is it worth it for me to travel to purchase this product and how far am I willing to go? Will follow-up service or support require more energy than I'm willing to give?

In their book *Emotion Marketing*, authors Scott Robinette, Claire Brand, and Vicki Lenz equate these purchasing values as points on a star. The symbolism helps set up the division between rational purchase drivers and emotional purchase drivers. In their example, they are able to draw a line dividing two of the points of the star from the remaining three, the line that separates the rational purchase drivers from the emotional ones.

rational   emotional

Product and Price represent the rational purchase drivers, these are the values we place on a product's quality, feature set, and price. Equity, Experience, and Convenience are emotional purchase drivers, they are the values we place on the brand as much as the product. Monster ideas rarely are formed on the backs of Product and Price. While rational purchase drivers are necessary to sell anything (no amount of advertising and marketing, emotional or rational, can make up for a crappy product or terrible price point), emotion still creates the strongest ties between product and consumer. Robinette, Brand, and Lenz would contend that a good product and comparable price point are the costs of bringing a product or service to market, a truth we have seen proven time and time again. (What's the last poorly made, shock-priced knockoff that you can remember that has inspired your patronage?)

My business partner, Mike Kelly, is fond of saying "The battle for market share is won and lost on an emotional level." What he's saying is that while product and price may sell in the short term, it's emotion that saturates over the long term. Emotion transcends rational purchase drivers, often initiating buying behavior or skewing rational purchase drivers in favor of a product or brand. While we all want to believe we are robotic in our ability to make the practical, rational choice, our humanity usually leads us to buy the brands and products that satisfy our emotional desires. Monster idea makers know this, they've formed their Frankesteinian creations to tap the unmitigated power of emotion and have witnessed firsthand the benefits of its wake. In short, rational purchase drivers are necessary components of the product's market existence, but emotional purchase drivers create a connection with that product that lasts. Monsters are emotional creatures (typically, they're portrayed as violently angry about something, but emotional nonetheless) and monster ideas are ones that typically use emotion to grow monstrous.

In 1988, Nike approached its heralded ad agency of six years, Wieden + Kennedy, to come up with the follow-up to Nike's successful "Revolution" campaign. Partner Dan Wieden went looking to solidify the effort with a memorable tagline, something they didn't create that often but seemed appropriate for this scenario. In the end, he turned to an off-the-cuff line he uttered in a 1988 meeting between his ad agency and the Nike marketing team. Wieden's monster idea: Just Do It.

"We felt we needed to have some cement to the thing," Wieden commented in a 1989 article for *The Oregonian*. "We felt 'Just Do It' would work for those at the competitive level as well as for people interested only in fitness."

While both the brass at Nike and the buying public weren't all that warm to the idea at first, the sentiment changed over time. As people began to make the authentic connections between the tagline and the character of the brand, the line became much more than just a company tag. It became a mantra. Peter Moore, the designer behind Nike's Air Jordan logo, admitted, "It was quick, easy, cocky, to the point, and a bit irreverent, all of which Nike is."

The Center for Applied Research (CAR) says the slogan is probably "one of the most inspirational brand statements of all time." By attaching itself to the emotion inherent in the athlete rather than the product, Nike can now sell athletic spirit in the form of whatever product they wish to peddle. Regardless of product or price, Nike stands for a can-do attitude, an attitude that most athletes either claim or desire to claim. This approach has nothing to do with the product and everything to do with the audience. It firmly grasps an emotional connection between the brand and the consumer but speaks nothing of the features, price, or quality of the product. When consumers are choosing between the myriad of athletic shoes they can buy, Nike has built an empire on the belief that they will choose the shoe that inspires them to act rather than a comparable shoe that sits squarely on rational drivers.

Monster ideas aren't always THAT monstrous. While all marketers would give their left pancreas (you don't have two?) to create something that has had such a worldwide affect as "Just Do It," the reality is the universe we can effectively alter is most likely much smaller. Thankfully, little monsters are often spawned from bigger monsters, allowing marketers to breathe new life into an idea's potential and create a monster in their own industry. We don't always have to reinvent the wheel, just the ride. Emotional drivers provide us the fertile ground needed to plant new communication seeds. Ad agency giant JWT came across this exact same scenario as they looked to make new what *Advertising Age* magazine dubbed "the best advertising slogan of the twentieth century," DeBeers' "A Diamond is Forever."

It's not often you find an advertising slogan lasting over 60 years, but when a young copywriter working for the first U.S. ad agency *ever* penned "A Diamond is Forever" for DeBeers, it's not hard to see why it stuck around. In 2008, JWT was charged with finding new conceptual ground for the emotional "forever" campaign. Their monster idea: The Unbreakable Kiss.   /UnbreakableKiss

DeBeers has had a long tradition of positioning itself in the marketplace as the actionable item clinging longingly to love. In the same way Nike understood that we, as humans, desire to act on empowerment, DeBeers understood that we, as humans, have a deep-rooted desire to act on love. By focusing on the emotion, the product that symbolizes that emotion comes along for the ride. In the case of DeBeers, the product is diamonds.

JWT was brought in to once again take this concept of love and marry that (pun intended. C'mon, that was good!) to the concept of "forever." Their monster idea came in the form of capturing the moment between two people when "forever" began. They erected an Unbreakable Kiss installation in New York's Madison Square

Park where people could come and document the kiss that started forever for them. Circling the installation were cameras, all set to capture the kiss from every angle. The resulting images were assembled into videos that resided on the diamondsareforever.com Web site where they could be spread virally via e-mail.

At first glance, the idea doesn't seem to have the chops to spread, does it? I mean, how many people could they possibly reach with such a one-to-one effort? What JWT felt, though, was the simple truth that people love to experience love . . . even when they're not involved. Why are chick flicks so popular in Hollywood? Because people watch them. We want to apply the emotions and scenarios to ourselves. (I mean, *chicks* want to apply the emotions and scenarios to themselves. I've never seen a chick flick, of course. I only watch *Gladiator* over and over.) We, as a society, are innately attracted to love. And sure enough, the idea grew monster when hundreds of thousands of people came to the site to experience captured moments of someone else's forever. News coverage expanded quickly and the campaign generated millions of dollars in free publicity for DeBeers. Not because DeBeers offers the finest diamonds at the lowest prices (although they might, my diamond market acumen is admittedly less than stellar. Don't tell my wife.), but because they authentically tied their brand character to the strongest emotion in the history of time to build what turned out to be a truly monstrous idea.

In the previous two examples, we've seen how empowerment and love can be springboards for monster ideas. But there are infinitely more emotions we can tap to carry our marketing and advertising ideas from good to great to gargantuan. Hope, fear, distress, surprise, guilt, shame, interest, excitement, joy, anger, disgust, contempt, sadness, happiness, peacefulness, grief, sorrow, trust, anticipation, depression, envy, frustration, sympathy, loneliness, embarrassment, horror, dread, awe . . . the available vehicles are too numerous to define completely. The key has always been to be authentic with the brand character. If you sell Mixed Martial Arts equipment, peacefulness may not be the most authentic emotion with which to tie your wagon (unless, of course, you're basing your idea on the most likely *result* of the less fortunate combatant). If you are raising awareness for protected wilderness sanctuaries, however, peacefulness may be a fully appropriate catalyst. Authenticity of emotion, therefore, becomes a key component to monster idea potential.

Consider, as an example, the emotion of nostalgia. One might desire to use this powerful emotion to market any number of products or services authentically, from picture frames to burial plots. But there's a secondary component to this particular emotion that plays a role in its effectiveness: age. Nostalgia, as an emotion, tends to be more powerful as we age. We experience more and naturally yearn for a time when we were younger, when the world was perfectly aligned with our reality. Ten-year-olds rarely yearn for "the good old days." But presented to the right audience and for the right product, nostalgia is an incredibly powerful emotion and one that can sprinkle monster dust on an idea.

Even Hollywood knows the monster potential of the right product mixed with the right audience and the right emotional tug. Don Draper, the worldly and well-spoken creative director for the fictional Sterling Cooper ad agency depicted in the 1960s-era AMC drama *Mad Men*, used the power of nostalgia in a legendary scene in which he pitched Eastman Kodak a campaign for their new "slide wheel" projector. In the pitch, Don Draper uses scenes from his broken life to emphasize the power of nostaligia:

My first job, I was in-house at a fur company, and this old pro copywriter, a Greek named Teddy, and Teddy told me the most important idea in advertising is new. It creates an itch. You simply put your product in there as a kind of calamine lotion. But he also talked about a deeper bond with the product: nostalgia. It's delicate but potent.

Teddy told me that in Greek, nostalgia literally means the pain from an old wound. It's a twinge in your heart far more powerful than memory alone. This device isn't a spaceship, it's a time machine. It goes backward, forward . . . takes us to a place where we ache to go again. It's not called the Wheel. It's called the Carousel. It lets us travel the way a child travels . . . around and around and back home again . . . to a place where we know we are loved.

As perfectly written as the dialog is, the lethal combination of slide projector and nostalgia would be lost on anything less than the perfect audience. The audience for that particular product is clearly an older audience, one that would collect family pictures or images of great sentimental value and yearn to show them. Even though this is a fictional example, it still represents a powerful idea carried on the back of authentic emotion.

So how would an emotion like nostalgia play out in today's world? Is nostalgia even a powerful emotion to today's consumer? Like the fictional example above, it completely depends on the product and the audience. So if you are sports drink staple Gatorade, and you're confronted with the startling statistic that only three in ten adults over the age of 30 exercise regularly, how do you sell more sports drinks to an audience that isn't engaging in sports? How do you reignite the athletic spark in this age group? You take them back to a time when they did. /Replay

Gatorade turned to their ad agency, TBWA\Chiat\Day Los Angeles, to tackle this problem. TBWA\Chiat\Day Los Angeles responded with their monster idea: "Replay." The agency developed an integrated campaign around the idea that there was a time when those who are over 30 and not exercising regularly did in fact find sports not only important, but life revolving. The agency used nostalgia to not only inspire action among the participant, but inspired action within those that experienced the campaign. Through this nostalgic experience, Gatorade became the brand that inspired a rediscovery of the sports and fitness lifestyle consumers once knew.

TBWA\Chiat\Day Los Angeles found two rival high schools that 15 years earlier ended their championship game . . . in a tie. They then went to the participants in that game and challenged them to settle the score . . . today. As all the participants are well into their 30s, replaying a full-contact football game could have been taken as far too dangerous, or met with little interest. But TBWA\ Chiat\Day Los Angeles knew what Gatorade knew . . . the athletic wing of the Nostalgia House is one that doesn't die easily. Not only did the players of that fateful game want to replay it, they wanted to train to do it right. As one would expect, they suffered through concussions, fatigue, exhaustion, and injury . . . and that was just in practice. The game was played in 100-degree heat but it did little to stifle the rivalry. The guys came to play.

Filmed documentary style, the Web-only content quickly grew monstrous, as more and more of this age group bonded with the notion of reliving a time in their lives when they were far more active. Gatorade sales grew within this age group right along with it. The idea grew so monstrous that Fox Sports Net picked up the idea and produced a season-long show restaging 15-year-old high school games, original contestants and all.

Nostalgia, accompanied by the right product and sold to the right audience grew an idea to monster proportions. The alternative rational purchase driver message simply couldn't have competed with the emotional connection. *Telling* those over 30 to exercise more and drink more Gatorade wouldn't have compelled action in the same manner. It was the emotion the campaign generated that carried the concept and created the monster idea.

That last sentence carries a word that we often overlook as marketers. It wasn't the emotion the campaign *communicated*, or the emotion the campaign *was based upon*, it was the emotion the campaign *generated*. There's a distinct emotional difference between telling and showing. In the Unbreakable Kiss example, if a friend were to be telling you about a Web site that documented the moment forever began for hundreds of couples, would it be enough to compel you to buy a diamond ring from DeBeers? Probably not (although if it is, you really should buy a few more copies of this book. No, you really should. Look into my eyes . . . you're getting sleepy, sleepy . . .). If you're in that 30+ age range and have exercised as little as I have, does just hearing about the campaign encourage you enough to get back in the gym? Taking it outside of the marketing and advertising world for a moment, do we authentically experience love from someone if they constantly say they love us but never show that love in any form?

> Monster ideas that truly evoke an emotional response do so because the emotion is generated, not just communicated.

In order for an idea to truly go monster, it has to be one that calls upon the emotion from within us, that allows us to put ourselves in the place of the subject. We have to be able to apply that emotion to our lives. From a marketing perspective, it requires us to have an understanding of our audience that goes beyond demographics. It's not about who they are but rather what they feel. When a brand can position itself as the remedy to a bad feeling, or the initiator of a good feeling, that brand can transcend rational purchase drivers. As consumers, we'll choose that brand over a brand that costs less or offers more simply because we *believe* in it. It's no longer a product, it's a cause. That accomplishment is difficult, certainly. It requires time and perseverance, but like Don Draper said, it's potent.

On the flip side of that, however, are instances when intended emotional responses are replaced with unintended emotional responses. This is a primary reason why so many marketers and advertisers choose to sit on rational purchase drivers over emotional ones: rational drivers are rarely wrong. There's little risk with telling someone that the product in question has more features or is priced comparably. There's also little reward, but often, the decision makers would rather sacrifice the potential reward in exchange for lessened risk.

Emotion is a powerful foundation to build upon and it requires an insight into the audience that many aren't willing to take the time and effort to discover. When this lack of intimate understanding of audience is coupled with a shallow attempt to draw upon emotion that may or may not exist within that audience, you can get embarrassing results. Think of it like dating.

You start dating someone but you'd really rather not get bothered by getting to know them all that well. It takes too much time. You just want them to be there when you need them, be around to go do stuff with, but getting to know who they are and what they like is a bit too much effort. So when you buy them gifts to "prove" how much you care for them, those gifts are shallow and impersonal, trinkets of little significance to the relationship. Then you decide you want to give them something nice, something they'll really like. You go down to the pet store and buy them a cocker spaniel pup. At dinner that night, you present the pup in a grand presentation that involved the waitress, the house band, and the other guests at the restaurant only to find out your date is deathly allergic to dogs and begins violently dry heaving upon seeing it.

Oops. Didn't see that coming.

This is what happens when marketers and advertisers attempt to generate an emotional response without an intimate understanding of the audience. Sometimes, we'll nail it on the head. Sometimes, we'll induce body-wide skin legions. It's a crap shoot.

In an attempt to generate the emotions of excitement and anticipation around the 2006 release of *Mission: Impossible 3*, Paramount Pictures had the idea to plant red music boxes inside 4,500 coin-operated newspaper dispensers in LA that played the catchy *Mission: Impossible* theme song whenever the dispenser was opened. The goal was to turn an everyday item like a newspaper dispenser into a mysterious, exciting mission. A good idea on the surface, certainly, but one that turned disastrously embarrassing when intrigue and excitement were exchanged for fear and anxiety.

The music boxes weren't well hidden within the dispensers, which made customers nervous. Calls were placed to the authorities alerting them of what some felt was an explosive in the newspaper dispensers.

Ahh, snap. Didn't see that coming.

John O'Loughlin, the senior vice president for planning at the *Los Angeles Times*, the provider of the newspaper dispensers, said "We weren't expecting anything like this. This was the least-intended outcome." The audience makes all the difference in an idea turning monster. If the only audience to patronize the newspaper dispensers were guys, ages 16 to 28, there's little doubt the response would have been the same. That audience understands the connection between the theme song and the newspaper dispensers, they, as a group, would have likely seen the idea as a clever initiator and the idea most likely would have accomplished its goal to excite. But the target audience for newspaper dispensers isn't 16- to 28-year-old guys. The audience is far broader, which lowers the chance for the idea to have the desired effect. The broader the audience that experiences the idea, the greater the chance to have not just ineffective results, but unintended consequences.

In 2007, Turner Broadcasting green-lighted a similar idea to increase awareness of a niche Cartoon Network show called *Aqua Teen Hunger Force*. The idea was to scatter almost 40 battery-operated Lite Brite-ish signs around downtown and suburban Boston featuring the characters from the show, some hanging from overpasses, some nestled against building walls, while others leaning harmlessly on light posts and street signs.

While the idea seems harmless enough, the issue isn't with the idea, it's with the audience. The show is geared toward 18- to 30-year-old guys. Boston is not made up solely of 18- to 30-year-old guys. So when residents of Boston are out walking about the city and begin to notice simultaneous appearances of aggressive characters flipping the bird built out of circuit board-looking devices surfacing in a major metropolitan area, fear outweighs entertainment. Calls came in from all over the city, reporting what many feared to be a terrorist attack. The bomb scare shut down the city for a spell while authorities and bomb squads were dispatched to reported sightings.

Sunuva. Didn't see that coming.

The originators of the idea were arrested (and when they were released, the media was waiting to ask them questions about the stunt, but they dodged all serious inquisitions by only responding about the history of certain hairstyles. "Were you contracted to perform this stunt?" "Hi, umm, we'd like to talk about hairstyles in the '70s" Hmmm . . .) Turner Broadcasting coughed up $2 million in fines and the CEO of Cartoon Network resigned. The idea generated emotion, certainly. Just not the intended emotion (unless the intended result was to scare citizens back into their homes where they may happen upon *Aqua Teen Hunger Force* on TV. Then it worked perfectly.). An understanding of not just the audience for which the idea is intended, but also the audience that may encounter the idea on the fringe will serve to help predict the monster potential of an idea.

So what happens when your audience can't be defined as acutely as you'd like? How do we generate authentic emotion when the audience is much broader than could possibly be researched? In those cases, it's vital to narrow down the list of possible emotions to those that are universal in nature. All of us, whether we're a 16-year-old guy in Southern California or a 60-year-old woman in Detroit, Michigan, desire and express certain emotions. We all covet love, we all experience hope or joy or trust. There are universal emotions that we can call upon that will mean more to certain groups but are at the very least universally experienced. Take longing, for example. We all long for something, most are specific to the individual, but there are universal longings most would admit to having. Like a longing to take a new job as the caretaker of a tropical paradise.

In 2009, Tourism Queensland came to ad agency CumminsNitro Brisbane to help them attract more tourism business to the Islands of the Great Barrier Reef in Queensland, Australia. The agency's monster idea: The Best Job in the World.

CumminsNitro Brisbane felt that the audience for this particular client was incredibly broad: a global audience of traveling vacationers. How do you reach such a broad target emotionally? You generate the universal emotions of longing and aspiration. They created a legitimate job search for what they called The Best Job in the World, the caretaker of the Islands of the Great Barrier Reef. The job requirements: Clean the pool, feed the fish, collect the mail, and report back to the world about their experiences. The job compensation: AUD $150,000 for a six-month position, live in luxury accommodations on Hamilton Island, and get the opportunity to explore all that the region has to offer. They were confident that if they posted a job ad for the best job in the world, people would apply. The agency placed the job in the want ads of every major newspaper in the world. Global news outlets picked up the story and provided AUD $400 million of free publicity. Thirty-four thousand people from all over the world applied.

A candidate was chosen from the thousands of applications and his island exploits were recorded for the world to see at the campaign Web site. The agency's modest goal was to generate 400,000 new Web site visitors over the life of the campaign. The monster potential of the campaign was evident after day one, when they amassed half that number after just one day. With two weeks left in the campaign, they had totaled 2.5 million new viewers to the site. In the end, the campaign has reached over three billion people through media coverage.

While the target of "everyone" is rarely an attainable goal, there are still universal emotional ties that relate to almost everyone. If we are able to identify these emotional truths, our ideas have a greater chance at turning monster. If you're looking to predict whether your idea has the potential to turn monster, one of the questions you need to ask is:

Will my idea generate an authentic emotional response?

MONSTER PARADIGM
EMOTION

Taking a look back at our Xbox 360 Halo 3 example, we can see how emotion played a significant role in the success of the campaign. To create a heightened sense of anticipation within their audience, McCann Worldgroup SF decided to take a game that was set in the future and create a campaign that was set even further beyond the time set of the game so they could speak about the battles within the game in the past. This used a peculiar combination of nostalgia and intrigue to create interest and desire. What happened in this battle? The only way to find out is to buy the game and play it. The idea creators desired to make the game more real by using real characters, humans documenting the actions of a fictional game hero. This accomplished what all first-person games strive to accomplish: put the player into the fantasy. In the end, the effective use of contrived nostalgia and dramatic intrigue connected the audience to the game by weaving fantasy with reality.

For example, in one online video, the documentary film crew that is used as the base for all interactions with the actors playing aged soldiers from the battle is set up in the Museum of Humanity, a fictional museum set decades after the battle supposedly memorializing the

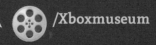 /Xboxmuseum

Human vs. Covenant battle. They are interviewing two former soldiers who are reminiscing about the battle and Master Chief. They are standing over a display of weapons and the documentary director asks the soldier if he would show him how the enemy weapon was held. The soldier reluctantly picks up the gun to demonstrate how it was held, and puts it down commenting that holding an enemy weapon feels wrong.

In another spot, another ex-soldier is at the Master Chief's gravesite, which is on the battlefield, reminiscing about the Master Chief and what he taught him. The soldier is staunch in his beliefs, even decades later, as he recounts the ceremony for the Master Chief as exactly that, a ceremony and not a burial. He makes a conscious effort to ensure that the director and the viewers know that Master Chief once told him, and he believes strongly still, that no soldier should be honored for doing what was expected.

/Xboxbattlefield

1

Does it evoke an emotional response?

TEAR PAGE

Emotional purchase drivers connect more
innately than rational purchase drivers.

Value is an intimate measure and is defined
in both emotional and rational ways.

Emotion can transcend rational
purchase decisions.

Authenticity of emotion plays a significant
role in effectiveness.

Emotion must be proven, not sold.

Knowing your audience ensures emotion is
connecting authentically.

It was May 19, 2001. An otherwise normal day in history, save for the genesis of the reinvention of retail but otherwise nothing of any historical significance occurred on that day. What's that? You're curious about the "reinvention of retail" thing? Oh, you already know about it. You've no doubt experienced it at least once in your life and I'm betting unlike other retail experiences, you can probably recall the particulars of the visit. It's not often a store becomes an attraction, but such is the case when you reinvent the retail environment and all. Still don't know where I'm going with this? Let me ask you a simple question, and I want you to *audibly* answer, as if I'm in the room with you. Don't worry that you'll probably garner puzzled looks and clandestine phone calls to anonymous authorities for talking to a book. The cover did that for you hours ago. Let me ask you this simple question and I want you to answer it aloud:

Which Apple Store have you been to?

I bet you can answer with a particular store in mind. I bet you can visualize what that store looked like, how you felt inside it, what was unique about it's architecture and design. I bet you can describe with some degree of detail what makes it different than other retail stores. Remember, at its core, this is a tech store, it sells computers and MP3 players and software just like any other gadget store. But it's the only tech store you can think of that's equal parts store and destination, retailer and hangout, seller and wonder. Why is that? Why is this experience so different than other retail environments

and how does it encourage customers to throw aside rational purchase drivers for the opportunity to be a part of its culture? The answer is simple in response but complex in meaning:

experience.

On May 19, 2001, Apple opened its first retail stores, one in Virginia and one in California. Since that time, Apple has opened over 300 stores worldwide and I'm betting you've been to at least one of them. If you haven't, dog-ear this page and hop a train or other overtly crowded public transportation vehicle and head to your nearest version. Also, you should move there. You'll be happier. Because within this retail environment you'll find a clearly underlying philosophy: people crave experience.

There are two types of experience that influence our behavior:

1. physical experience
2. brand experience

As marketers, we often mistake the two as "either-or" entities but in terms of monster idea potential, it takes both working together to accomplish monster results. The Apple Store concept exercises both in spades, which we'll explore. What's interesting about the Apple Store experience is that this philosophy isn't hidden or shielded from the customer. The brand character Apple has communicated is very open about experience being its primary selling mechanism. We, as consumers, know what the goal is: to sell us Apple products. And yet we welcome that goal openly in this environment where in others, we put up a wall that says "You cannot *sell* me anything, I will choose when I am prepared to *buy* and any attempt to woo me otherwise will be met with sharp rebuke." (Okay, you may not say that exactly, I fully recognize the word "rebuke" is a weird word to speak, but you get the picture.) The key to Apple's store experience is that both the brand experience and the physical experience work in harmony to create a thoughtful, human retail habitat.

The brand experience at the Apple Store mirrors the philosophy Apple was born from: create lifestyle. Apple has come to symbolize simplicity and the intangible "cool" factor of living a digital lifestyle. While others were touting processing speed and computing power, Apple spent their energy promoting pictures of the kids, videos of family outings, and portable music. Apple didn't start with consumer's computing needs and look to meet them, they started with people's lifestyle wants and looked to enhance them. What was a complex process on other systems became child's play on a Mac. Apple's brand character is one of simplicity, lifestyle, and design. The Apple Store mirrors that brand character in the form of tangible experience.

As Apple has become accustomed to doing, they reexamined every part of the retail experience to see how they could reshape it to fit their brand character. Take the checkout process for instance. In most retail environments, the checkout process begins when the customer enters the checkout line. Apple, on the other hand, believes that the checkout process begins when the customer has decided to buy. The time between that buy decision and the act of paying is a dangerous time. The more time that passes between the buy decision and the credit card, the likelier it is they could change their mind, so Apple equips an abundant staff of eager employees with portable credit card swiping checkout machines. Apple brought the checkout line to the customer: Simplicity.

Each of the products Apple sells at the store reinforces the lifestyle Apple has created. Don't know what that lifestyle means to you? Ask one of the 673 customer service reps who seem to be just standing around. Why are there so many employees on the floor? Because Apple knows that the lifestyle they are creating is amplified to the customer the more the customer knows about the product, and what it can do for them. The floor reps are trained to be both friendly and knowledgeable. The philosophy is to make themselves available for the consumer when the consumer has a question, not constantly shadow and confront about a possible purchase.

For his book *Punching In: One Man's Undercover Adventures on the Front Lines of America's Best-Known Companies*, author Alex Frankel spent some time as an Apple Store employee. He documents Apple's philosophy on customer service and how that differs from other retail environments. "At an Apple Store, workers don't seem to be selling (or working) too hard, just hanging out and dispensing information. And that moves a ridiculous amount of goods: Apple employees help sell $4,000 worth of product per square foot per month. When employees become sharers of information, instead of sellers of products, customers respond." This "sharing of information" rather than selling goods, directly parallels Apple's business philosophy: Lifestyle.

Apple products have been widely acclaimed for their aesthetics as well as their engineering. The team at Apple takes great pride in producing products that look the part as much as perform the task. Sleek, stylish, and simple, Apple's design philosophy plays out in the Store environment equally well. From the maple veneer tables the product is displayed on to the ample room for gathering and exploring the product offerings, the Apple Store environment is designed to be clean, efficient, and most of all, comfortable. It's not about getting you in and out as fast as possible, it's about giving you time to explore the lifestyle as much as the products. In the end, the store is just as much a desirable gathering place as it is a retail establishment: Design.

These brand experiences remain authentic in the store because the physical experience serves to enforce them. It's one thing to *say* you have a lifestyle-driven philosophy but it's an entirely different thing to actually *prove* it. The physical Apple Store experience, from the design of the store to the interaction with the employees to the policies of the environment, the physical experience is out to prove that Apple is set apart.

How many stores that you can think of are actually designed for you to loiter? The Apple Store not only tells you to stay as long as you like, they mean it. You can hang out all day if you want, check e-mail, browse the Web, write a book. No, not me (although I am currently hunting and pecking on a Mac), a woman by the name of Isobella Jade who wrote nearly 300 pages while coming to the SoHo Apple Store on a daily basis during 2005. Not only was Jade not shooed out of the store, she was welcomed, with employees even making special efforts to close down the computer she was using last so she'd have more time to write come closing. She would bring stacks of notes and enough grub to write for a few hours a day. To further prove the act was more policy and less apathy, they asked Jade if she'd do an in-store reading of the manuscript a few months later. Imagine another retail environment that not only *permits* daily dawdling, but *encourages* it.

The buzz within the Apple Store is palpable, partly because it's rarely empty. That's what happens when you design a retail experience to feel more like an event than a store. Products become shows, and value is prescribed in terms of what the consumer becomes more than what the product provides . . . the hallmark of any emotional consumer relationship. Employees don't hover, they're smiling, T-shirt-clad kiosks of information just waiting for you to approach them. The Apple Store even includes what they call "The Genius Bar," a place for customers to come to ask tech support questions and get anything and everything Apple fixed. How many other consumer tech brands offer a *physical place to go* for tech support? Apple understands the easier it is for consumers to understand the lifestyle Apple offers and the products that support that lifestyle, the easier it will be to sell them more products. The physical experience celebrates this understanding.

So, what can we learn from the Apple Store about experience and how does that translate to monster potential in our marketing and advertising ideas? How does a retail experience relate to marketing? First and foremost, the Apple Store represents an immediate touchpoint to the brand. You not only experience the brand character, the cult of Apple right there in the store, but you can try the product firsthand. And not just the product, but how all the products work together. Trendwatching.com, the independent online consumer trend network, dubbed this concept "tryvertising," or "the integration of a product or service into daily life in a relevant way so that consumers can make up their minds based on their experience, not marketing messages."

What better way to communicate that Apple's products indeed live up to the lifestyle hype than to let people try them for themselves? While certainly not a novel concept ("tryvertising" has been around for decades, think free shampoo samples at grocery stores or product placement in hotel rooms), the monster idea potential of "tryvertising" has unlimited experiential possibilities. If the product or service in question is the real deal, any opportunity to prove that to potential consumers is an opportunity to create a monster idea.

Ever wonder what that particular shade of lipstick would look like on you? Or that one, or that one? (I haven't, of course. Except for this one time in college, but everyone was experimenting back then, right? There's a "Stefanie" in all of us, that's what I keep telling myself.) L'Oréal wants you to find out. In 2010, the makeup giant tested the "tryvertising" market in the UK by installing a series of digital "mirrors" that allow potential customers to test makeup without actually applying it to their skin. Consumers use the kiosks to take a digital picture of themselves, then scan in the barcode of the products in question to see how they would look when applied. The kiosks also will allow prospective customers the ability to select different colors of the products, even get advice on the perfect shades for a customer's skin tone or eye color. This augmented reality provides a product experience previously unavailable save for actually applying the product.

Then there's the Dutch-born Senseo Coffee Maker, a one-cup coffee generator whose producers know a thing or two about the difference between saying and showing. There's few aromas more powerful in the morning than the scent of coffee. To business travelers and coffee fanatics alike, it's virtually impossible to initiate a morning sequence without that magic elixir. So if you're trying to make waves in a crowded coffee maker industry, how do you differentiate yourself while taking advantage of a sensory experience most advertising and marketing mediums fail to support (smell and taste)? You create a targeted experience with your product and become the brand that understands what their audience wants most.

In 2009, Douwe Egberts and Philips, the development team behind the Senseo Coffee Maker, installed coffee machines in bus and tram stops all over Sweden. Doesn't sound like too monster of an idea, but consider that the installations featured the stylish design of the actual coffee makers and that the coffee was free to the travelers waiting for their morning transportation and you can imagine the idea potential. The two greatest sensory experiences coffee can provide, smell and taste, are immediately communicated to the exact target audience that would benefit most from a one-cup coffee maker.

In each instance, we can see it was a combination of brand experience and physical experience that led to the monster idea. The concept of self-application is vital for experience to be effective, we need to be able to apply the product or service to ourselves to fully appreciate the emotional significance. In short, if we can't see ourselves in it, no amount of messaging will convince us otherwise.

> Experience is an active expression, it provides a marketing vehicle that brings the brand to the consumer but does so in a way that still allows the consumer the ability to form the interaction.

The L'Oréal digital mirrors brought the brand to the consumer in the form of product trial without product commitment, but the consumer was still in control of the interaction, they could choose what shades, what colors, and what products they desired to see. If the purpose of advertising is to incite a positive action toward a product or service (or simply sell more product, for the more direct-minded), is there a better method of advertising than the consumer actually using the product? (Only if the product doesn't suck, I suppose.) After using the L'Oréal digital mirror, how many people would be able to admit that they had just seen an ad for L'Oréal makeup products? Few would categorize their experience as being advertised to, but that's exactly what occurred. The brand character and message was conveyed, they spent time with the brand and were able to envision themselves as users of the product. Ask any marketer what they'd hope to achieve with any marketing or advertising efforts and you're likely to hear a similar response as a hopeful outcome.

When an experience is created, and the brand is brought actively to the consumer, the experience provides "ad cover," a method in which consumer's ad radar is lowered and they become more susceptible and accepting of marketing messages. If you're a Jeep Wrangler kind of person, you're willing to accept any and all Jeep Wrangler marketing messages, regardless of how aggressive they may be. You've already bought into the culture, you no longer need to be convinced of their merit or require convincing of the desirability of their culture. They're preachin' to the choir, so to speak (doubly so if you're actually in a choir and drive a Jeep Wrangler). Your ad radar is all the way down.

In contrast, if you're out looking to buy a car and not interested in a Jeep at all, any attempt to sway your opinion toward a Wrangler feels intrusive unless that attempt is offered to us under the cloak of experience. By creating experience, we are wrapping the brand message and desired consumer action in an activity or exchange that rewards the consumer for their time, whether that be product sample, interaction, or entertainment. Experience provides an emotional, tactile exchange that marketers typically attempt to convey through traditional, passive communication channels. From something as small as Amazon's "Search Inside" feature that allows interested book buyers a preview of the book's contents in an effort to duplicate the brick-and-mortar bookstore experience to something as large as guests at the Ritz-Carlton being provided a Mercedes-Benz CLS500 with unlimited mileage for the duration of their stay, a full tank of gas each morning, and overnight valet parking to show off the features of the luxury automobile to their target audience. In the end, it's human nature to be skeptical of what we're told by advertisers and marketers and believe what we experience for ourselves.

When you have a product or service that sells itself, the monster idea potential exponentially increases when marketing and advertising ideas put that product or service into the hands of the consumer in a memorable way. If you're Procter & Gamble, for instance, and you have a luxury toilet paper in the form of the Charmin brand, you'd want people to (clear throat) try out (clear throat) the product to prove how luxurious it really is. So you can send your target audience a roll as a "tryvertising" example, but your audience is, well, everyone with a bum and a buck, so that may be difficult to do. Plus, how memorable is a roll of toilet paper in a mailbox anyway? Doesn't really fit with the brand character, and doesn't really provide any memorable experience to the consumer. Instead, you'd want to meet the consumer where they are, when they need your product and service most. You'd want to mirror that luxurious brand character but stay authentic to who and what you are: toilet paper. Their monster idea: Charmin Luxury Restrooms.

Public restrooms in and around the Times Square area of New York don't exactly have a reputation for being clean, luxurious experiences. On the contrary, you have a better chance at contracting previously unknown strains of exotic viruses than not, so Charmin installed a 20-stall public restroom in the heart of Times Square called the "Charmin Luxury Restroom." Open from 8 AM to 11 PM to capture the Broadway show crowd leaving the theaters, the restroom offered clean, deluxe bathrooms, baby changing stations, stroller parking, sitting areas, and even the presence of a bathroom attendant for every two stalls, cleaning the stalls and restroom after every use.

While you may not remember a roll of toilet paper arriving in the mail or handed to you at a store, you're certain to remember the time you left the show late at night and desperately had to go use the john, only to find the Charmin Luxury Restroom available to you, providing a slightly less than presidential restroom experience. And that experience is what you will associate with Charmin the

chasing the monster idea │ does it create an experience?

next time you walk the toilet paper aisle in your local grocery store. The unexpected nature of the experience (the presence of a clean, luxurious, free public restroom in Times Square), in conjunction with the authentic brand exchange (Charmin is a luxury toilet paper) given to a focused chunk of your target audience (theater enthusiasts and tourists who more than likely have the means to choose a luxury toilet paper over lesser-quality, lower-priced competitors), and combined with the media exposure something of this creative ilk naturally procures led to this unique monster idea.

The aspect of the Charmin idea that shouldn't go unnoticed in its success was the authenticity of the concept. Take a dirty place, add a touch of cleanliness and luxury and make that dirty place wonderful for a small period of time. That's what Charmin is promoting with its brand character (you can define "dirty" however you like), so the experience it created worked because it was in line with its character. If the idea was simply to put Charmin toilet paper in the elegant restrooms of upscale Manhattan bistros, the connection would have been less powerful. It was the transformative quality of the environment that made the idea so authentically monstrous.

Authenticity is often difficult to transport, especially if your goal is to find an authentic way to not be salesy and pushy with your product or service. Advertising and marketing, by its very nature, is a push industry. It's our job to get people to react, recognize, and remember. But being authentic doesn't always have to be about the product, service, or brand. If our product or service is designed to help people accomplish something, maybe being authentic is to simply recreate that act. This is exactly what British ad agency AKQA did for search engine Yell.com. Their monster idea: Results for Real Life.

AKQA noticed that Yell.com had a robust local search usage, so they developed the Results for Real Life campaign to promote how Yell. com could help people find the places they wanted to go *while* they were going there. They installed interactive screens at bus shelters that highlighted local shops, restaurants, and bars to help users find their way *on their way*. The kiosks were powered by and branded by Yell.com, providing a valuable service experience users would take with them long after they arrived at their destination.

Along with these knowledgeable bus shelters, AKQA also developed the world's first GPS advertisements on London buses. Yell.com sponsored 25 buses equipped with LED panels that display messaging matching the bus's geographical location, all based on GPS technology. The effort branded Yell.com as not only a smart, local search engine, the campaign positioned Yell.com as the expert in the local scene, in *whatever* local scene the user happened to experience the interaction, customizing the experience for consumers by presenting the very service they provide as an unexpected, authentic real-life experience.

While experiential ideas don't always involve nontraditional marketing tactics, bringing the brand to the consumer where they are least likely to expect advertising often means developing unconventional communication vehicles because those places are often not prepared to provide traditional marketing messages (a firm grasp of the obvious I have. And evidently a propensity to talk like Yoda.). Many of the most monstrous experiential ideas involved ideas that fell outside of what we'd consider traditional marketing methods (any place or media we are accustomed to experiencing advertising messages). Over the past couple decades, we've seen more and more successful campaign incorporate a level of a-traditional, experiential marketing. The industry slang for this type of idea is called "Guerrilla Marketing."

The term "Guerrilla Marketing" was coined by Jay Conrad Levinson in his 1984 book *Guerrilla Marketing*. In it, Levinson defines guerrilla marketing as "achieving conventional goals, such as profits and joy, with unconventional methods, such as investing energy instead of money." The application of this is best described as nontraditional marketing tactics that take the campaign message to the consumer through time, energy, and imagination rather than big marketing dollars. The idea is to maximize the impact of the message to get as much bang for your buck as possible. Many would classify guerrilla marketing as nothing more than PR stunts, which is partly true, but a well-executed guerrilla marketing plan can turn an average idea monster quicker than traditional media alone.

Guerrilla marketing tactics, like all experiential marketing strategies, are intimately tied to the strength of the concept, the knowledge of the audience, and the understanding of the role of emotion and authenticity in marketing communication. Like any other form of advertising, a poorly conceived guerrilla marketing tactic delivered to an unreceptive audience can backfire. The same qualities and characteristics we hope carry our message to the consumer can act as our downfall as guerrilla marketing tactics tend to be remembered, passed along, and talked about. If that tactic misses the mark, the same communication channels and viral tendency will serve to pass along the failure in the same way it would have passed along the success. So guerrilla marketing is not the magic pill some hope it to be. Simply showing up is not enough. The strategy, concept, execution, and audience are just as vital to the success of guerrilla marketing techniques as traditional advertising channels.

Examples of guerrilla marketing can be as small as "reverse graffiti," a street tactic where marketing messages are placed in urban areas by removing the dirt or grime from a surface rather than adding to a surface with paint, ink, or paper. The Salvation Army used such a technique within their Portland, Maine, "Free Ad Space" campaign in 2009. To raise awareness and donations to the charity, the Salvation Army hit the streets of Portland, Maine, to secure as many free or donated ad spaces as they could muster, including strategically parked cars with messages written by finger on filthy windows. The campaign centered around the familiar Salvation Army icon, the shield, and messaging that creatively reinforced the truth of free ad spaces contributing to the Salvation Army's donation reality: "83 cents of every dollar donated goes directly to the people who need it most." The Salvation Army found a way to be authentic with their message without compromising the delicate balance between donations and ad spending. A truly monster idea.

If you're a public aquarium who just went through a multimillion pound refurbishment and want to get the message out about the new experience visitors can have at the aquarium while continuing to push for environmental conservancy, a slightly twisted use of "reverse graffiti" might be in order. London SEA LIFE Aquarium had just this challenge. Their monster idea: Sea tagging.

The aquarium tapped media agency Curb, whose environmentally friendly guerrilla marketing tactics had become something of English marketing lore over the last few years and included such guerrilla marketing monsters as sand sculptures, turf cutting, and an ingenious campaign for the sports and lifestyle brand Extreme that involved tagging natural snow drifts with 3-D stencils in and around London. This time out, Curb developed the idea of sea tagging to communicate the experiential nature of the London SEA LIFE Aquarium. Understanding that salt water evaporates more slowly than fresh water, taggers in scuba suits hit the streets of London and using custom sea life stencils, like turtles, dolphins, and whales, the team sprayed salt water through the stencils onto buildings, sidewalks, and surfaces all around the city. The images lasted for as much as 15 minutes and left nothing but a small seasalt dusting when they evaporated. No permits required and an experience that is both conceptually authentic and executionally memorable.

Ad agency Leo Burnett Frankfurt used the "reverse graffiti" concept for Tide detergent in an equally authentic way. Instead of removing dirt from urban surfaces, they waited for the dirt to arrive. Along a busy German street in 2008, the agency constructed a long, sparkling white poster made of cotton. At one end was a Tide logo and nothing else. That is, until the natural dirt and grime you'd imagine would build up on a cotton poster along a busy highway arrived over the course of a few weeks and revealed what appeared to be a clothesline stretching from one end of the poster to the other . . . knocked out in white where they had applied a stenciled portion of the cleaner. The resulting tag line appeared next to the Tide logo as well: Longer Lasting Whites. The concept of time was authentic to the brand message of longer lasting whites, as was the appearance of the white clothing silhouettes and cotton material. Monsterlicious.

Guerrilla marketing can also be executed on a grander scale. The cost to impact ratio begins to blend on larger scale guerrilla tactics, and Jay Conrad Levinson himself would probably question the size aspect, but impact is certainly relative to the size of the budget so larger scale guerrilla tactics, while graying the line between traditional and nontraditional, certainly have merit.

Ad agency TBWA\180 and adidas got together to add a mix of traditional billboard media with guerrilla spirit when they entered the ad space of the busiest pedestrian intersection in the world in Tokyo, Japan, to stand out from the most cluttered outdoor market on Earth. How do you stand out, stay true to your brand mantra, "Impossible is Nothing," and communicate an authentic brand exchange in a memorable way? Their monster idea: Vertical Football.

/VerticalFootball

For adidas soccer, TBWA\180 produced a billboard with a soccer field covering the length of the board with three-dimensional goals at both ends. Nothing spectacular or noteworthy, until you suspend two live players from ropes from the top of the board, suspend a ball and ask them to play live 20-minute matches to the shock and surprise of the pedestrians below. News outlets the world over pick up the offering, and a monster is born.

In 1999, half.com, the used merchandise online marketplace, was suffering from a crowded Internet-naming syndrome and was looking for a much needed shot in the PR arm. How do they get the media attention to help bridge the gap between the marketplace and their name, which speaks nothing of what they provide? Their monster idea: Half.com, Oregon.

Half.com approached the small town of Halfway, Oregon, and paid them $100,000 (and a new computer lab) to legally change their name to half.com for one year. Roadsigns were changed, addresses were edited, and the residents were now residing officially in a town called half.com. News outlets ate it up and half.com got the PR boost they so desperately needed. So successful was the campaign that global Internet retail giant eBay gobbled up the small company for $313 million.

While the gargantuan guerrilla efforts are less prevalent and begin to stray from the spirit and purpose of guerrilla marketing, most guerrilla marketing efforts fall somewhere in between. The desire to bring the brand message to the consumer so they can experience it in an unexpected and memorable way leads many brands, and the agencies that represent them, to develop guerrilla tactics as part of an overall campaign. The goal with any effective guerrilla marketing tactic is to draw on the power of showing, not just telling.

Ad agency Indie Amsterdam created such a campaign element for Domino's Pizza. Armed with the understanding that most people order pizza to be delivered to their home or office, Domino's wanted to communicate that as long as consumers are within delivery range of a Domino's Pizza, they can have a pizza delivered virtually anywhere—on the beach, in a park, on a boat . . . anywhere. Their monster idea: Domino's Delivery Points. /ManHungry

The agency developed a series of white doors, complete with door frames, doorknobs, and doorbells. These doors were placed in heavily trafficked public areas like beaches, parks, and promenades, adorned with signage that informed passersby that they could order Domino's virtually anywhere. If consumers ordered from the doors, delivery drivers would even ring the doorbell on the installation to alert the consumer that their delivery had arrived.

Often, these ambient tactics are part of a larger campaign to draw attention to the product or service in a way that becomes even more memorable than traditional media infiltration alone. Such was the case for Folgers Coffee, who hired Saatchi & Saatchi to develop a campaign for their flagship coffee brand. As part of a greater campaign, the agency added a guerrilla tactic to take the message to the consumer in the form of vinyl manhole covers.

Placed around busy New York streets, the agency covered street manholes that spewed steam from the heat below through the ventilation holes on the cover. The vinyl overlays provided a bird's-eye view of the top of a cup of hot coffee, now steaming from the manhole, and the message "Hey, City That Never Sleeps. Wake up. Folgers."

Ad agency Publicis of Malaysia did something similar with their client, HP. To promote how vibrant and realistic HP's photo paper is, the agency developed what looked like human-size black holes ripped out of paper. They strategically placed these black holes at places within the city that had a defined transition from one environment to the next. The illusion was that the cityscape behind was actually printed or fake, and that people were walking through the hole to get by when in actuality, the only thing fake was the hole. Closer inspection of the hole propped in its strategic location revealed the HP photo paper ad.

Guerrilla marketing tactics are an effective method to bring the brand character and message to the audience and provide an experience that drops the audience's "ad guard" so messaging can be communicated effectively and willingly. As part of an overall marketing and advertising effort, and in conjunction with the appropriate strategy, concept, execution, and audience, experiential efforts such as guerrilla marketing tactics have been proven to produce lasting consumer effects. If you're looking to predict whether your idea has the potential to turn monster, one of the questions you need to ask is:

Does my idea create an authentic brand experience?

MONSTER PARADIGM
EXPERIENCE

When we apply the idea of experience to our Xbox 360 Halo 3 example from the introduction, we see a campaign that has a foundation of experience. First, a primary creative execution of the "Believe" campaign was to use real human "war veterans," set in the future beyond the game's time set, to reminisce about the battle and Master Chief's role in the war. This creates an immediate relationship with the viewer and sets the campaign up to weave in and out of real-life drama and video game fantasy.

/Xboxdiorama

Second, a key aspect to the game was the availability of a 1,200 square foot diorama that was developed at 1/12 scale and depicted the battle between the humans and the enemy in the game, the Covenant. This diorama was actually produced and the miniatures provide amazing detail to the battle that would come when the game arrived. Web site visitors could pan the length of this and zoom in to scenes to imagine what was occurring and what they'd be a part of when the game was launched.

Last, an underrated aspect to the launch was an Alternate Reality Game. The ARG executions involve a similar weaving of fantasy and reality, bringing fictional environments and characters into the real world so fans can extend the fantasy of the game. In the case of the Xbox 360 Halo 3 campaign, this game was code named "Iris." It started when the public beta of the game had concluded. A seeded user in the Halo 3 online forums alerted game zealots to a Circuit City-planted ad that was leaked that revealed a Web site where an interactive comic was housed. This comic could be manipulated to reveal the IP addresses of a series of secret Web sites that housed secret societies from groups within the game, as if they were real and posting content on the sites. The ARG component cemented the strategic direction the agency developed to weave fantasy and reality and provide an experience to potential consumers that couldn't be experienced through traditional advertising and marketing channels.

Does it create an experience?

There's two types of experience: brand experience
and physical experience.

Monster marketing and advertising ideas require
authentic representation of both.

Experience brings the brand to the consumer in
unexpected and memorable ways.

Self-application is vital to developing
effective experience.

Experience offers a chance to prove
brand character, not just tell it.

Guerrilla marketing is a form of experience,
bringing brand messaging to the streets
to convey a message inserted into
consumers' everyday lives.

WELCOME TO

Luckytown

MISSOURI

THE **LUCKIEST** PLACE ON EARTH!

You wake up to yet another perfect morning. It's 72 degrees and sunny . . . just like yesterday. And the day before that. And the (insert any time period marker) before that. The birds are chirping the flowers blooming, and the only thing blue is the sky. You ge your perfectly temperatured cup o' joe and head out to your fron porch to get the paper. The headline news of the day: "For The 763rd Day in a Row, Nothing Bad Has Happened." You smile as you wave to the newspaper kid as he delivers a perfect strike from his shiny new bike to the front porch of your neighbor, Dave. Funny he wasn't even facing Dave's porch but the kid never misses. Dave': the perfect neighbor, by the way. Pulling from years of experience as both a Horticultural Artist and Recreational Vehicle Inventor, his hedges are always manicured perfectly and often in the shapes o fictional movie characters or brands of microbrews and he always seems to have an extra turbocharged, twin cam, solar-powered houseboat laying around that he'd love for you to use. Or just have Lord knows he has another. Yep, this is your neighborhood, and it': fantastiglorious.

As you get dressed in your custom-designed Armani tank top and 12 and 3/8th sized Gucci sandals, you decide to go into town to pick up a few essentials: Some eggs, milk, a new set of diamond-milled irons and your own personal orbiting satellite. The 197" plasma yo just installed in your "between 6 PM and 8 PM" room gets fuzz reception on channels 12,546 and 12,547 so it's time to replace tha five-person satellite you've been sharing with the Guthries and ge your own. As you pass the playground on the corner where the kids are tooling around in their 1/8th scale Maseratis, you can smell the aroma of Mrs. Kelly's chocolate chip cookies. Oh, man, there's little better than her cookies. Ever since she cultivated her own coco-farm and processing center, the chocolate tastes like it was grown on trees. She offers you a basket as you cruise by, you can see the steam coming from under the silk towel covering the morsels of nirvanic enchantment. You can't resist. Who could? She's actually not that good of a cook, she sets the oven to "whatever" when she bakes but it just seems no matter what she does, she gets the perfect batch of cookies every time. "Thanks, Margaret. You rock."

After launching the satellite and picking up the eggs and milk from Brian's Grocery and Spa, you're feeling as groovy as ever. The whole "massage while you shop" concept is heavenly, but now you have to get down to the gym. The high school boys varsity basketball team is putting their 187-0 record on the line against a pretty tough opponent. You pay the girl at the ticket counter with another twelfth century gold doubloon and find your seat on the goose feather bleachers. You're late, the game's almost over and it's a squeaker. You wish you hadn't stopped for those cookies, you'd have loved seeing how the 131-6 score got so close, but so be it. "C'mon Blue!" you scream, and sure enough, we hit another buzzer beater to fend off a feisty adversary. Whew.

As you head back to your humble-casa-slash-medieval-castle, you pass another moving truck pulling into your neighborhood. It seems the block is growing by leaps and bounds, new folks are filing into Luckytown by the droves. That's what they get for winning the Missouri State Lottery, a ticket to Luckytown, the luckiest place on earth. Yep, this is your neighborhood, and it's fantastiglorious.

You want to go there, don't you? Who wouldn't want to live in Luckytown, the luckiest place on earth? If you had a chance to get a ticket to Luckytown, you'd throw a dollar down, right? That's exactly what ad agency Barkley Evergreen & Partners were counting on when they created Luckytown for the Missouri State Lottery in 1998. They were counting on saddling the emotion of hope with the reigns of entertainment, and that this cowboy would lead to increased lottery participation in the state of Missouri during a time when most lotteries and other state-run ventures were cutting back spending.

Entertainment is the hallmark of memorability in the marketing and advertising industry. In an effort to make a brand message or character stick in the minds of consumers, marketers often turn to entertainment as the glue. Jon Bond, cofounder of ad agency Kirshenbaum Bond & Partners, once said, "Telling and selling doesn't work as well as it used to because I'd literally just tune out the commercial. Because of that, the merger of entertainment and selling is inevitable. Unless there is entertainment value, why would I opt in?" The assumption is that if the messenger entertains the audience, they are far more likely to remember the message. Think of it like a singing telegram (sidenote: whatever happened to singing telegrams? This seriously is one industry that needs to make a comeback. Who's with me? Okay, nevermind.). If you were going to visit a forgetful friend back east, and you sent a singing telegram to his door announcing in song the day and time of your arrival, he'd probably have an easier time remembering to pick you up at the airport than if you just sent him an e-mail or left a message on his voicemail. The idea is the messenger plays just as significant a role in the memorability of the message as the message itself.

But there's a fine line between entertainment and relevance, a line that many advertisers and marketers fail to see. Monster ideas aren't ones that simply entertain, they're ones that entertain with relevance. If you sent that singing telegram to your friend's door, and that messenger broke into a killer rendition of Lady Gaga's "Paparazzi" then left, as entertaining as the messenger was, he failed to deliver the most important thing: your arrival day and time. Entertainment for the sake of entertainment isn't advertising. It's entertainment. Even famed ad man David Ogilvy once said, "I don't regard advertising as entertainment or an art form, but as a medium of information." Advertising may not be entertainment in and of itself, but without entertainment, advertising has little chance of spreading in today's culture.

"Luckytown" was a monster idea because the high entertainment value in the campaign was directly tied to the campaign concept of hope. To get more people to play the lottery, Barkley Evergreen & Partners developed a campaign that revolved around the desire people have to win anything, to be considered "lucky." Any amount won gets you a fictional ticket to the fictional Luckytown, a place that people not only relate to on an aspirational level, but desire to be on a relational one. Even though everyone knew it was a fictional place, the agency created a connection between the material dreams of Missourians and the lottery in a way that remained memorable. Senior copywriter on the campaign, Tug McTighe, said, "People no longer were just passively playing the lottery, they actively looked to punch their ticket to Luckytown. It became more than a point-of-purchase decision, they sought it out. The entertainment value in the campaign influenced behavior, that's what good advertising does." The campaign was both entertaining AND relevant. Without the relevance, the entertainment factor would have been temporarily amusing, but would have had no lasting marketing effect.

The primary creative goal of the Luckytown campaign was to begin to treat the Missouri Lottery like a brand. The creative team behind the effort, VP of Integrated Marketing Jeff Fromm, Associate Creative Director John January, Senior Art Director Paul Diamond, and Senior Copywriter Tug McTighe, felt that in order to use entertainment in a relevant way, they first had to create character in the brand. "Great brands have a personality," Fromm said, "and what we've done is give the Missouri Lottery a personality. We wanted to capitalize on the feelings a customer has when buying a lottery ticket."

The campaign included traditional and nontraditional elements to stretch the entertaining direction and begin to exercise the emotional and experiential aspects of the campaign. They teased the campaign before launch, introducing some of the residents of Luckytown, including a local curmudgeon who has a beautiful girlfriend and another man who was hit with a gold meteorite. They released 30-second spots like "Coach," where the head football coach of the Luckytown University Leprechauns recounts in true "ignorance is bliss" style how his undefeated 85-0 squad has bumbled and lucked their way to success. "Retailers were being called 'Luckytown travel agents,'" January said, "and the winning number drawings were 'Live from Luckytown.' Radio stations even began referring to their broadcast reports as 'reporting from Luckytown,' no matter where they were in Missouri." The campaign spread because the entertainment factor was directly relevant to the target audience and the brand character they were developing simultaneously.

Entertainment, however, is a slippery slope. What's entertaining to one person may not be to another. That's why relevance, both in message and audience, matters.

Monster ideas often use entertainment as a carrier but never at the expense of relevance. They find what is authentic to the brand character and audience to go from good to great and great to monsterlicious. Especially in advertising and marketing, humor seems to be the entertainment du jour. It's hard to think negatively about something that made us laugh or smile, so advertisers have been trying to put a smile on consumers' faces for decades, all in the name of brand or product recognition. Historically, entertaining campaigns like the Budweiser Frogs, Jack-in-the-Box's ping-pong-ball-headed CEO or "Got Milk" (plus one or two or 432 million others) have all used humor as an entertainment focus and been pretty darn successful doing it. But the ideas that go monster are the ones that find a rare mix of entertainment and pertinence in their makeup. "The two places to err in a commercial are all entertainment and no selling or all selling and no entertainment," Kirshenbaum Bond & Partners' Bond also said. "Everyone watches and nobody buys anything or nobody watches. Finding the overlap is the issue." /SiennaCampaign

One great example of a campaign that found that overlap and it turned the idea monster was the 2010 Toyota Sienna campaign from Saatchi & Saatchi LA. Minivans haven't been cool since . . . well, never. But that all depends on your outlook, or so we would be led to believe by the creative team behind Toyota's minivan offering, the Sienna. Dubbed "The Swagger Wagon" within the campaign, the minivan becomes the symbol for style and swagger . . . if you're a mommy and daddy. Erich Funke, Creative Director for Saatchi & Saatchi LA and lead on the project said, "The insight actually came from studying the vehicle, and reading through the 'design intent' from the Toyota engineers. From this, it became clear one of the important points-of-difference was this minivan has really cool styling. (For all too long, the minivan has been completely about the kids. But the Sienna minivan is different. Sure, it has all the bells and whistles the family unit needs, but styling-wise, it was obvious it was made with the parents in mind.) Parents often sacrifice their own wants and needs for their children's, and often the biggest example is their purchase of a minivan. What we did is flip the script on this thinking; we wanted to show today's parents that owning a minivan doesn't mean they need to be fitted for mom jeans (or immediately banned from Facebook)."

The entertainment value comes in the form of personal relation. The audience is obviously families, and with that comes mommies and daddies who once thought they had some street cred but now have taken a different role. By bringing some of the street cred back in the twisted form of self-importance, the campaign and the product both inherit a heightened place in the minds of the audience. The more you relate to the characters and their plights, the more you see yourself in the scenario, making a direct application to the product. /SiennaTimeout

In one TV spot, the Sienna's luxury is petitioned through the mom desiring to spend as much time as possible in the car, away from the craziness of family life. She's shown talking on the phone to her girlfriend, watching the dual-panel entertainment center and sleeping, as if she's at a spa or in the sanctuary of her bedroom. She notes at the end of the spot that "I tell my husband the more time I spend in it, the less stressed I feel. And the fewer headaches I get" followed by her husband quickly pulling their car-door-knocking daughter away from the car so the wife can rest quietly. Other spots involve the dad taking the kids to a playdate only to find another dad "copping his style" with the unveiling of his own Sienna or the mom commenting that the stylish nature of the minivan results in folks often mislabeling her as "the hot babysitter." /SwaggerWagon

One of the most talked about arms of the campaign is the music video shot with the family. The rap parody, "Swagger Wagon," documents the life of these Sienna owners with lines like "I got a swing in the front, treehouse in the back, my #1 dad mug says, ya, I'm the Mac." and "I love hangin' with my daughter sippin' tea, keep my pinky up, all the drawin's on my fridge scored an A+." Shot entirely in black-and-white and a hardcore rap style mocked fluently throughout the piece, the online-only video has had almost 6 million views so far. The comedic nature of the piece in conjunction with a relevancy to both the product and the audience from the content of the effort has turned the idea monster and done what all commercial campaigns strive to do: go viral.

One of the harbingers of an idea turning monster is its ability to go "viral," or when the organic online social networks grab something that entertains and compels and they spread the content digitally. Going viral is when people pass along your messaging for you, and it's the goal of any marketing effort, but it's also the hardest to predict. Entertainment plays a pivotal role in the naturally organic nature of viral content, which makes it an unpredictable goal. We naturally look to pass along content that we found entertaining, but not necessarily relevant. If it's funny, we'll be more apt to pass it along, but the end goal of brand messaging becomes secondary to entertainment, a dangerous place for advertisers and marketers to live. Like David Ogilvy said, we create information, not necessarily entertainment, although we use entertainment as a vehicle. What goes viral is really up to the fickle masses, despite any marketing efforts to sway the course. In short, marketing efforts that rely solely on "going viral" typically fall short of their expectations.

The very act of digital dissemination as a viable marketing result may have started in earnest in 1999 with the arrival of the *Blair Witch Project*, the low-budget horror flick that spent almost nothing on formal marketing, instead relying on a Web site that seemed to document the happenings within the movie as real life. This grayed line between fantasy and reality led people to spread the word with their friends and the movie turned monster when the $22,000 production budget (including marketing) parlayed into $248 million at the box office on word-of-mouth alone. But from a marketing and advertising point of view, it was Crispin Porter + Bogusky's "Subservient Chicken" Web site for client Burger King in 2004 that opened a new frontier for advertising and marketing's view of the power of viral.   /SubservientChicken

The agency was given two key directives: promote Burger King's new TenderCrisp Chicken Sandwich and stay within the brand character established and marked by the tag line "Have It Your

Way." The result was a Web site, subservientchicken.com, that featured video of an actor in a chicken suit set in a bland apartment living room. The viewer could type into an input field a command, and the chicken would respond to the command, performing the act defined by the command. If someone typed "Do a little dance," the chicken would dance, if someone typed "hop up and down on one leg," the chicken would do it. The viral nature of the campaign came into play as people tried to stump the chicken to do something outrageous based on the commands, but few people could command the chicken to do something that he couldn't do. As people e-mailed their friends and word-of-mouth started taking over, the campaign turned monster. The entertaining nature of controlling a video of a man in a chicken suit seems silly, but when you consider the conceptual tie between having the new chicken sandwich and "having it your way," the campaign's monster potential was huge.

Other successful campaigns have used humor as entertainment and found viral gold. In 2010, ad agency Wieden + Kennedy introduced a former NFL wide receiver to the world as the monster idea "The Man Your Man Could Smell Like," and Isaiah Mustafa will now and forever be known as the "Old Spice Guy." /OldSpiceGuy

Old Spice has an obvious stigma to overcome. They're old. They smell like spice. They're old and spicy. They make us all think of our grandpa. But brands like Gillette and Axe were kicking Old Spice's spice, so something had to be done. Old Spice desired to appeal to a younger demographic, that 20-something crowd of guys that had responded bodywash-favorable to the metrosexual push of the late '90s with a hearty "No, I'm not! (yes, I am.)" If Old Spice could make a run at this group and steal just a little market share, they could see the transition coming and continue to work on the group. Wieden + Kennedy went to work on the brand, releasing spots starring Bruce Campbell, Neil Patrick Harris, Terry Crews . . . even Jackie Moon made an appearance (thanks to Will Ferrell and his entirely too-tight shorts, of course). And as entertaining as these spots were, it wasn't until "The Man Your Man Could Smell Like" hit the Web that the campaign really turned monster.

The TMYMCSL spot (if I have to spell it out, reread the last paragraph and write 100 times on the board "I will understand the acronyms") started out with Mustafa's soon-to-be signature line "Hello, ladies" in that deep Barry White-esque voice. He then goes on to document that while the ladies in the audience may wish their men looked like him, they couldn't, but they could smell like him if ladies bought Old Spice bodywash for their men. The tag line "Smell Like a Man, Man" concludes each spot.

The spots are written extremely well, and are certainly entertaining. But entertainment alone wouldn't be enough to make a dent in the stigma the agency needed to overcome, they simply couldn't reach enough of the targeted audience to influence sales numbers with TV spots, regardless of how entertaining they might be. So in an effort to combine entertainment with relevancy, Wieden + Kennedy took to the place the audience spends an inordinate amount of time, online, and they developed content they felt would be worthy of a viral result. And in the process, they redefined the standards for possible reach of viral content.

The original TV spot was no Internet slouch, mind you. After six months, the original spot reached 18 million views. Considering that the average age of Internet users in 2010 was 26, that's a decent number of people in their target to view the spot. The follow-up spot, in the same time frame, garnered 14 million views. So the TV spots were pulling an amazing number by themselves. Armed with a natural understanding of Internet culture and Mustafa himself in studio, the agency set out to do something incredibly unique and right in line with the brand character they'd established with the spots: they filmed live responses to questions to the Old Spice Guy on various social networks, from Twitter to Facebook to Digg. As TMYMCSL answered questions, the team quickly processed and uploaded the responses to the YouTube channel they had created for the spots, to the tune of 181 video responses in a 24-hour period. Clad in his traditional towel and rippled pecs, the Old Spice guy answered questions about his love life, what he does for fun, how President Obama could be more manly, and he even proposed for a Twitter follower. He answered questions from Internet celebrities like Digg founder Kevin Rose, blogger Perez Hilton, and even groundswell chat board behemoth 4chan, whose followers number in the hundreds of thousands and has the power to shape the digital opinion of a vast number of the target audience.

/TMYMCSL

The results were astounding. In a single day, the YouTube channel pulled 6.5 million viewers, Twitter followers went from 8,000 to 70,000 in a two-day period, and Facebook fans jumped on to the tune of almost 32,000. The total brand reach in the first six months of the campaign has topped 110 million views.

The viral success of the TMYMCSL campaign can be directly attributed to the combination of entertainment and relevancy. The spots are well executed and appeal to a broad range inside the target audience while the immediacy of social networks added the much-needed layer of relevancy. Without one or the other, the campaign wouldn't have enjoyed the level of success it has earned. If the spots weren't that entertaining to begin with, no amount of social consciousness would encourage the audience to share it with their networks. If it's not funny, why pass it along? If the campaign hadn't used the social stratosphere to produce the immediacy of that entertainment, a large number of potential customers would never have had the brand exchange and experience Wieden + Kennedy hoped to generate. It took both. Monster ideas always do.

Take, for instance, a struggling import beer who found a 22 percent increase in sales over the same four-year period that the import business as a whole *lost* 4 percent. The reason for the success? It tends to reason that if anyone could convince guys to put down their lesser-priced domestic beer and pick up your imported brand, it would be The Most Interesting Man in the World. /XX

The creation of ad agency Euro RSCG New York, The Most Interesting Man in the World eloquently hawks import brand Dos Equis and has been doing so with a flare one would expect from someone that has led such an interesting life. The spots take one of two paths: either a narrator dead panly unfolds interesting facts about TMIMITW's life (again with the acronyms, GAWSH!) or TMIMITW provides a pearl of wisdom about a variety of topics.

The narrated spots are incredibly well written and pattern themselves after the popular Internet meme of Chuck Norris ("Chuck Norris' tears can cure cancer. Too bad he never cries." or "Chuck Norris doesn't sleep. He waits.") by unveiling the remarkable-slash-absurd life TMIMITW has led, like "He once had an awkward moment, just to see how it feels" or "He can speak French—in Russian" or the popular "If he punched you in the face, you'd have to fight off the strong urge to thank him." The B-roll is grainy and homespun, giving the illusion that he's only captured on film by the unprepared few, usually engaging in some ridiculous act, like playing jai alai or steering a motorized fishing boat full of beauty pageant contestants. The spots end with the same line, delivered from the grizzled TV veteran Jonathan Goldsmith: "I don't always drink beer, but when I do, I drink Dos Equis. Stay thirsty, my friends."

The spots that include Goldsmith providing advice to the viewers on a variety of subjects are just as entertaining. In one spot, TMIMITW sits at a bar table, surrounded by beautiful company, and waxes poetic on subjects like careers ("Find out what it is in life that you don't do well, and then don't do that thing."), or life ("It's never too early to start beefing up your obituary."), or even pick-up lines ("There's a time and place for them. The time is never. You can figure out the place on your own."). These versions typically end with just "Stay thirsty, my friends."

The spots are, naturally, entertaining. Where's the relevancy, you ask? It's in the audience. As marketers, we often turn to spokespeople that represent our audience, or who we think they want to be. How often do we turn to who they aspire to be seen as? Former Chief Creative Officer at Euro RSCG New York, Conway Williamson, says that's exactly why the campaign has been so revered. "When they get to the bar, they want to tell a better story about the life they lead," admits Williamson. The Most Interesting Man In The World is what the 21- to 34-year-old guy wants to be, relevant.

Another aspect to this relevancy is a small but consequential part of the campaign. It's rare in marketing or advertising for a brand to openly advertise that their spokesperson doesn't always consume the product in question. At the end of the spots, TMIMITW admits "I don't always drink beer, but when I do, I drink Dos Equis." The natural inclination is to say "I'm the most interesting man in the world, and I always drink Dos Equis," but the agency knew that wasn't how guys authentically chose which beer they'd purchase. Guys, like TMIMITW, don't always drink beer and this authenticity made them more relevant to their target.

Add to the spots a Web experience that contains hundreds of other characteristics of TMIMITW, social networks that provide a forum for fans to create their own characteristics and a variety of games, like arm wrestling famous world leaders of yore and an alternate reality game where players search for TMIMITW's lost cargo (lost in transit from a mysterious, exotic foreign country, of course), and you have an integrated campaign that reaches beyond the borders of the TV to connect with the audience where they reside. Another monster idea born from entertainment and relevancy.

While humor is most often chosen as the entertainment of choice among marketers and advertisers, it's not the only type of entertainment that has produced monster ideas. In 2001 and 2002, BMW launched *The Hire*, a series of eight Internet short films that were released on the BMW Films Web site, a branded content portal for the auto maker. Back at the beginning of the decade, video was still widely underused on the Internet, as transfer rates were still considered too low for the sharing of video-related content. Bucking that statistic, the extremely popular Web series starred actor Clive Owen as the "Driver" and were directed and produced by popular filmmakers from all over the world, like Guy Ritchie, John Woo, and Ridley and Tony Scott.

The purpose of the series was to showcase the features and characteristics of the BMW line of automobiles, but was done so in dramatic (and sometimes explosive) fashion. Each of the films were stand-alone short stories and roughly 10 minutes in length. After the series launched in 2001, BMW saw a 12 percent increase in sales from the previous year. In a time when the Internet was still in its infancy, the four-year period that BMW Films existed saw 100 million brand views.

/ParallelLines

Speaking of Ridley Scott and short films, his studio, RSA, was approached by ad agency DDB Worldwide for their client Philips in 2010 to take on a branded-content project called "Parallel Lines." The concept was created to communicate that there are millions of ways to tell a story, but there's only one way to watch one . . . on a Philips TV with their Ambilight technology, award-winning picture quality, and superior sound. "Parallel Lines" takes one piece of dialogue and asks five different filmmakers within the studio to create a short story that uses that dialogue to serve the primary objective. The result was five very different films, all using the same dialogue: "What is that? It's a unicorn. Never seen one up close before. Beautiful. Get away, get away. I'm sorry." The fertile filmmaking ground the dialogue provides created a remarkable playing field for the accomplished storytellers, and they created an interesting and entertaining mix of emotions, from joy and wonder to sadness and self-realization.

Entertainment isn't a new concept for advertisers and marketers, certainly. But as the media landscape changes almost overnight, how relevant entertainment is to the intended audience plays a significant role in its effectiveness as a marketing vehicle. It's one thing to be funny or thought-provoking or awe-inspiring, it's an entirely different animal to be funny or thought-provoking or awe-inspiring authentically within the character of a brand and within the character of the target audience. If you're looking to predict whether your idea has the potential to turn monster, one of the questions you need to ask is:

Will my idea authentically and relevantly entertain my audience?

MONSTER PARADIGM
ENTERTAINMENT

In our Xbox 360 Halo 3 example campaign, it's easy to see the entertainment value in the spots McCann Worldgroup SF created. What's interesting to note, however, was that the spots didn't rely on humor as the entertaining characteristic. The game is about a battle, a war that occurs in the future. To be authentic to the brand, the creators developed a series of spots and Internet video content that treated the battle the way we would treat a battle—with dignity and respect and reverence. The combatants in that battle, therefore, would inherit those same qualities. This was a primary undercurrent to the campaign, this reverence of the game's main character, Master Chief. The spots were entertaining not because of their humor or wit, but because they again skirted that line between reality and fantasy.

The other point of note about the campaign was the depth to which it went to "sell" the story line. Fantasy is fickle, it requires the shelving of reality for a time and those who weave fantasy know how fragile the state can be. The creative team went to great lengths to further the fantasy for they knew that anything less would test the fragility of the fantasy and they risked exposing the strings on the marionette to the audience.

3

Does it entertain?

Entertainment is the hallmark for memorability in the marketing and advertising industry.

Entertainment for entertainment's sake, however, is NOT advertising. It's entertainment.

Relevance gives entertainment its effectiveness as a marketing vehicle.

Relevance comes in two flavors: Relevant to the brand and relevant to the audience.

Entertainment doesn't always mean humor. As humans, we are entertained in many ways.

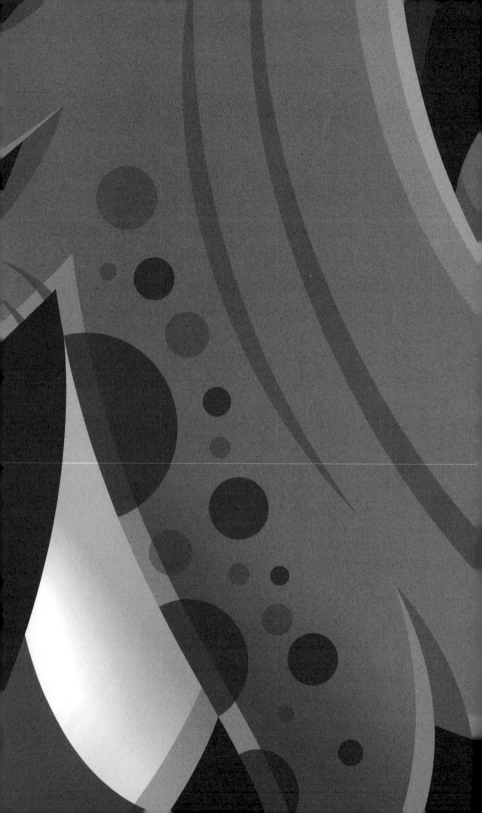

4

Is it novel?

As you walk into the clinic waiting room, you can't help but feel like a human guinea pig. You immediately regret the decision to answer that UCL Institute of Cognitive Neuroscience ad in the paper (". . . but Ma, the ad is so interesting and different, I can't get it out of my head! I feel compelled to take their study," you said. "Do what you want," she said, "but don't blame me if you come home thinking you're a goat."). You take a seat and pick up that May 1972 issue of *Boys' Life* that's calling your name from the table. A quick gander around the room finds a similarly regretful-looking group of what you can only assume are others who felt similarly compelled to take similar actions. Damn, that ad was so similarly compelling!

On a seemingly regular interval of time, a nurse steps through the swinging gateway door, butchers someone's name and leads them inside, the victim . . . err . . . study participant usually taking one last look behind in case they, too, come back through those doors craving the fresh taste of grass. Each, though, seemed to have emerged from the experiment decisively human and none the worse for wear. Almost happy (read: relieved). Then, Nurse Namebutcher calls your name (or a facsimile thereof) and you step through the doors and into the study room. Modest enough, the study room feels quite academic, outside of the fMRI scanner used to analyze your brain activity. You know, that old chestnut.

The study seemed harmless enough, and you really didn't even have to do anything but look at a bunch of pictures. Many of the pictures were nice, pictures of people smiling and laughing and photos of the outdoors, like hills with green pastures (although you immediately thought of your mother's goat inference when the grass came up and you wondered what the analysis was going to read about that.

Off, sir . . . he thinks he's a goat."). Many of the images were the exact same as pictures you'd been shown previously, like they were testing your memory or something. They even dropped in some not-so-nice images in the mix, like pictures of car crashes and people's faces when they were angry or screaming. But then, every once in a while, they'd drop in a new image you hadn't seen, something distinctive and cool. But mostly, they'd mix up the order and show you pics of scenes and faces you had already seen, some multiple times. You had no idea what they were studying, you just wanted one (or eight) of the free bite-size candy bars you saw in the basket on the way out.

You left the study feeling less like a goat and more like a pig. And not the guinea variety you originally thought, thanks to Nurse Namehatchet and her never-ending supply of "take as many as you like" candy bars. No, the other kind.

Okay, chances are you didn't have that experience. The story was fictional (what!?) but the study was real. In 2006, researchers from the UCL Institute of Cognitive Neuroscience did indeed conduct a study on novelty and its effects on memory. What they discovered has long been hypothesized by marketers and advertisers for years: Novelty has a profound effect on motivation, reward processing, and learning.

The researchers were studying a region of the midbrain which is responsible for regulating our motivation and reward processing. These are especially interesting areas to marketers and advertisers as they influence buying behaviors, what ultimately motivates us to make a purchase decision. Study participants were involved in a series of experiments like the one described in our story, using images and recurrence to test brain activity. The results of the test led researchers to conclude that brain activity and memory were both heightened when new images were introduced in comparison to familiar images, or ones they had seen before. The response to new images was even measured higher than the images that evoked a strong emotional response, like the pictures of angry faces and car crashes. Dr. Emrah Düzel of the UCL Institute of Cognitive Neuroscience said, "When we see something new, we see it has a potential for rewarding us in some way. This potential that lies in new things motivates us to explore our environment for rewards. The brain learns that the stimulus, once familiar, has no reward associated with it and so it loses its potential."

Marketers and advertisers have long felt that novelty, or the state of something being new or original, was an effective, if not essential, aspect to marketing success. The study's conclusions serve to reinforce this philosophy, certainly. If our ability to remember a product or service or brand message is increased by the novelty of our experience with that product or service or brand message, it tends to reason we, as marketers, should be actively seeking novelty within our ideas. As advertising and marketing ideators, we're constantly searching for ideas that we can say, "Well, THAT'S never been done before." Certainly, many of the monster ideas we've explored so far in this book have novel components to them that set them apart and make them memorable in the minds of consumers. But looking at the study, was it really heightened memory that has the greatest reward for advertisers and marketers looking to defend novelty as a viable marketing approach? Dr. Düzel's quote carries an interesting focus right in the middle of the pull: "This potential that lies in new things motivates us to explore our environment for rewards." Motivating us to explore our environments for rewards as a by-product of novelty speaks less to memory or brand retention as it does to something far more powerful: curiosity.

If you take nothing else away from this exploration into monster ideas, take out your monster highlighters and give this a big slab o' yellow:

Curiosity is the most powerful marketing force on the planet.

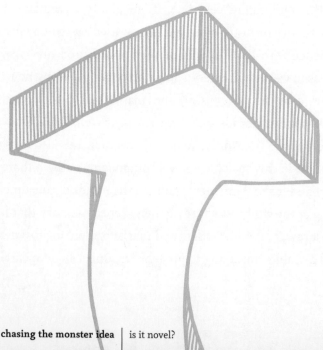

Curiosity leads us to explore that which we don't know. It's technically categorized as an emotion rather than an instinct, which is particularly notable because instinctual reactions are typically more defined (If I jumped out from behind this book and screamed like a banshee at you right now, your instinct would be to retract. It would be incredibly rare for fright to be met with another action. But on an emotional level, after you've retracted, you may laugh at the fact that I scared you, or you may cry from the scare, or you may punch me in the neck. All emotional responses, all valid. Except the punch, that hurt.). Emotional reactions, however, vary from person to person. This means we, as marketers, can hope to evoke subtle to blatant emotions with the marketing messages and messengers we choose to employ. Curiosity, as an emotion, is something we can hope to enact within our audience for the purposes of encouraging them to explore our brand character further.

I know what you're asking: Why would I care more about curiosity than memory? I want potential customers to remember my brand when they are in a buying state of mind. While that may be true, the difference is one of will. With memory, we may remember your brand, but can't recall why. And worse, we can't recall what we're supposed to remember about your brand because memory isn't always a matter of will, we don't always *want* to remember something, we just do. Ever get a song stuck in your head all day? Chances are, it's not a song you want to remember, you just can't shake it. (I will say to you Culture Club, now good luck getting rid of "Karma Chameleon" all day. You can loathe me later.) You probably don't have positive feelings about the song when four or five hours go by and you're still humming verses, either.

But curiosity can't exist without will. You have to *want* to know more, to explore further. When we are curious, we are investigating something we don't know for the single purpose of knowing. Our goal is to understand, to remember. Moreover, when we are curious to know something, and we gain the knowledge we need, it's difficult not to look fondly upon the learning experience because we ushered it. If our ideas can inspire curiosity, we are being given permission from the audience to further the brand revelation. Even more so, they're *actively* inquiring to know more. It innately creates attention, something marketers and advertisers would give their art director's right arm to procure.

Novelty is only a useful tool if it creates curiosity, but as a tool to do so, is more motivating than any other characteristic. If we can provide an experience that the audience sees as new or original, we have a naturally curious occurrence. Market research firm Yankelovich Inc. tells us that the average adult is exposed to over 5,000 advertising messages per day. Holy cow! I'd ask you to recall right now how many advertising messages you've seen today. Take a moment to list them out. I'm betting you can't actively recall more than 10, and if you can, I'm betting there is an element of novelty to a good portion of them. We are inundated with marketing messages, how can we possibly encourage rogue memory let alone curiosity? Originality or novelty plays a definitive role in what we retain.

But originality comes in many flavors. It can be as big as a new medium or as little as an original headline. It can be groundbreaking, never-before-seen in any industry or a slightly modified version of something that we are innately familiar with. In the end, novelty itself isn't the attraction. It's what we choose to make novel that turns ideas monstrous.

Infamous ad man Leo Burnett once said, "The secret of all effective originality in advertising is not the creation of new and tricky words and pictures, but one of putting familiar words and pictures into new relationships." He was saying novelty isn't about finding something new under the sun, it was making something we find familiar new to the audience we seek to influence. That's what the state of New Mexico was counting on when they introduced their monster idea, wait for it . . . talking men's urinal cakes.

To help curb the rise of drinking and driving in the state of New Mexico, the southwestern state issued new urinal cake technology to bars and restaurants all over the state (urinal cake technology being so slow to growth, evidently). The urinal cakes would warn unsuspecting, umm, "patrons" with a warning at a time when they perhaps were most vulnerable. "Hey there, big guy. Having a few drinks?" says a female voice a few seconds after an approaching male sets off a motion sensor in the device. "It's time to call a cab or ask a sober friend for a ride home." Jokes aside (like that's easy), the campaign was a monster success. As drunk-driving reports fell, bar patrons statewide openly admitted the novelty of the urinal cakes caused them to think twice about getting behind the wheel.

Urinal cakes aren't new (it's hard to believe that sentence has ever been published before, but there you go). Anti-drink-and-drive messages aren't novel. Even talking bar products aren't original (the animatronic fish on the wall would like to join in another chorus of

"Karma Chameleon" with you. Just couldn't let it die, could I?). But like Leo Burnett implied, it's finding the novelty in what we already find familiar that makes something original and interesting. I would reckon (did I say "reckon?") that there were few guys who weren't curious about the urinal cakes and their message. When they left the restroom to tell their buddies, their stories would be considerably less interesting (and most likely chalked up to drunken stupor) if they came back with "Hey, fellas, the toilet talked to me and said stuff." The novelty of something they've experienced every day being transformed to serve a new purpose is novelty enough to turn a good idea (passing along a drinking-and-driving warning) into a monster idea.

It's completely common, however, for marketers and advertisers to become enamored with the thought of originality. How often do we downplay a good idea because we feel like "it's been done before." While I personally believe that there are still unexplored frontiers to be uncovered, Leo Burnett is still right. Originality is just as much in finding new relationships as it is finding new frontiers. The key, like anything, is to be authentic to the brand character and the audience. Noted designer Terry Marks once wrote, "Be true, and original will not matter an iota." This seems in conflict with the notion that novelty is a characteristic of monster ideas but the reality is it's in perfect concert with the philosophy. Marks isn't saying not to be novel, he's saying don't make novelty the priority in an idea. Look for ways to be novel through the filter of brand fidelity. This filter is present in virtually every monster idea we'll encounter, and it's a precursor to predict monster potential in our own ideas.

Take our old friends Crispin Porter + Bogusky for instance (think "Subservient Chicken" from our chapter on entertainment). The ever-churning creative minds at CP+B were searching for yet another social network coup for their client, Burger King, and decided to create a Facebook app to promote the fast-food chain's signature fare, the Whopper. Facebook apps have been a hit and miss proposition in the advertising world. Most efforts failed to use the social media for anything more than a transparent media mechanism but the Facebook app that CP+B developed was counting on something a little bit more in tune with the social mentality. Their monster idea: The Whopper Sacrifice.

The agency developed a Facebook app that has a very simple but novel premise. Instead of asking for friend requests from Whopper enthusiasts, they went the other way: defriend 10 people from your friends list and get a free Whopper. The catch: your recently hatcheted unfriends will get a notice that you've chosen 1/10th of a Whopper over them. Ouch.

/WhopperSacrifice

That's really all there is to the effort. Simple, effective, and novel. Simple in that the campaign requires no other actions to be taken. You do this, you get that, end of story. Effective in that the Facebook app was installed almost 60,000 times in less than a week, close to 20,000 Whopper coupons were delivered which means over 200,000 Facebook friends were axed in exchange for a burger. All this for little to no marketing dollars being spent on advertising for the app. Novel in that CP+B turned the idea of social behavior on its head and relied instead on the entertainment value of an already familiar notion, friending and defriending. The agency made something original out of something familiar.

The campaign success numbers provided are only for 10 days because that's how long the campaign ran—10 days. Not because of any strategic decision, but because Facebook disabled the campaign after 10 days claiming it was a violation of privacy rules on the social network. The app alerted people when they were defriended. "Some people thought it was a little brutal because we did send notifications," Matt Walsh, head of the Interaction Design department at CP+B, admitted. "If I defriended you, you would get a message saying that you were worth less than one-tenth of a Whopper." Sacrificed or not, the Whopper Sacrifice campaign got just as much buzz out of being axed as it would have if they had become Facebook's BFF.

Staying in Facebook's sandlot, stylish but ridiculously DIY furniture giant IKEA turned to Swedish ad agency Forsman and Bodenfors to help promote a new store opening in Sweden's new heptagon-tooled hot spot: The city of Malmo. The new Malmo IKEA was captained by store manager Gordon Gustavsson, an important character in the agency's campaign. Charged with getting the word out about the store opening, the agency turned to Facebook to distribute the news. Their monster idea: Gordon Gustavsson's Facebook Photo Album.

/IKEA

The agency created a Facebook profile for good ole Gordon, then promptly filled his photo album with images of IKEA showrooms, those vignette-heavy room pods so prevalent in the way IKEA features its furniture on the showroom floor. The images showed beautiful room designs with every piece in the image available from IKEA.

If this were the end of the promotion, there's little chance word would have spread sufficiently. While beautiful, catalog images are hardly novel enough to warrant viral potential. But when a common, familiar action on the popular social network is applied in a novel way, good ideas turn monster in a hurry.

The agency added one small instruction to the pics that changed everything: if you're the first to tag an object in the photo with your name, you win it. So the first person to tag the couch gets the couch. If you tag the vase, you get a dandy new flower receptacle free of charge. Every gallery photo in his album is fair game. Tag it, get it.

That one instruction started an avalanche of attention for the store and the brand. People willingly spread the word through their profile, links, and chatter (even though technically, wouldn't your chances to score something increase if you kept your mouth shut? Just sayin'.). Gordon became a bit of a cyber celebrity, with fan requests for insider scoops on new images being uploaded and questions about the store. The idea turned monster for the grand distribution total of $0. Or krona, depending on your currency of origin. A novel twist on a familiar experience.

Novelty is often found when authenticity meets opportunity. As fortune cookie-ish as that may sound, the truth is that it may only take an observant eye to find monster potential in the everyday. If you're a cell phone manufacturer and you want to take advantage of absurdly massive gatherings of your target audience, you may decide that music festivals, concerts, or sporting events are an excellent opportunity to reach a large number of people with a target brand experience. "Oh, snap," you say (I doubt you said that, but this is a family title) "music festivals are super loud, how can we have a meaningful brand exchange when we sell an audible communication device?" How about Nokia Silence Booths, a branded cone of silence from which ear-smashed festival goers can make a call in peace and quiet. Finding silence at a music festival, how novel.

Or if you're a beer brand and you want to get folks out in quantity to where their beer is sold, you may look around and find a monster idea is right there for the taking. Dommelsch beer stumbled over a monster idea in the Netherlands in 2006 when they adorned cans, bottles, and coasters with bar codes that could be entered on the Dommelsch Web site to find the secret dates and locations of the next pop-up concert featuring well-known artists and big name acts. The small venue, big artist concept went over so well, they expanded the campaign to include supermarkets where Dommelsch was sold as venues. That changes grocery shopping night, doesn't it?

In the chapter on experience, we spent some time exploring guerrilla marketing and nontraditional, experiential advertising. Many guerrilla marketing tactics rely on novelty as the backbone of campaign creative, putting the shock value of experiencing a campaign in unsuspecting places on the back of the brand message. If novelty really does evoke curiosity as an emotion, providing a place for potential consumers to experience the brand in a novel way makes sense. It becomes especially original when the brand character of the product or service meets an otherwise familiar experience.

Grey Worldwide in Germany was charged with bringing the Toys 'R' Us brand to potential consumers in a playful, novel way. One campaign execution brought their inflatable beach toy collection to the public by converting an ordinary bulletin board advertising column one may experience on a walkway into the blow up spout of an inflatable globe beachball, as if it's the blow up spout to the Earth itself. A sign placed on the spout simply read "Inflatable Globe, €9,99."

Uber-successful HBO crime drama *The Sopranos* didn't need much marketing help to reach the pinnacle of television viewership, but they rarely disappointed with their efforts. One such effort used New York cabs as guerrilla shock value when select taxis around the city, something often seen in and around New York (did some of my sarcasm splatter on your shirt?), were fitted with fake arms dressed appropriately in gangster black shirts and gray jacket sleeves hanging out of the trunks. A simple bumper sticker accompanying the whacked hooligan simply read "Sopranos. Only on HBO."

In 2010, Panasonic asked ad agency AKQA London to help promote their new Lumix ZX1 digital camera with 8x optical zoom. One element of the campaign involved making life-like sculptures of everyday objects and placing them in inconspicuous spots where those objects, like pigeons, orange traffic cones, etc., may normally be found. Except those objects weren't life-size, just life-like. In fact, the objects were 8x larger than normal, potential consumers could experience for themselves what it's like to be 8x closer to an object. All the sculptures led consumers back to the Web site where they could submit their own pictures of what happens when you use forced perspective and the Panasonic Lumix ZX1.

These are all examples of creating novelty from familiarity. None of these ideas by themselves are original but combined with an evocation of curiosity among the audience, monster ideas were formed. In each case, the character of the brand was the primary message and the subject of the novelty, with the Panasonic ZX1 taking it one more step and shining a purposeful spotlight on the actual features of the product or service. The spotlight strategy provides fertile ground for novelty but with a notable caveat. If the take away from a particular marketing or advertising idea can both be entertainingly original AND communicatively informational, monster ideas can form. This method, however, has been hit and miss in the advertising and marketing industry. Often times, the effort is far heavier on information and too light on novelty. This makes the fact that this is an ad with the intention of altering consumers' behavior come to the forefront and the "ad radar" gets put on high alert. It takes a keen sense of character to develop product or service-centric features in an authentic yet novel way.

Imagine, for example, your creative product is . . . creativity itself. You're a copywriter, an advertising copywriter, that is. Your job is to be as creative as possible. That is, when you have a job. Lots of brilliant copywriters are out of work, the least of which was certainly not Alec Brownstein. This creative copywriter had to find a way to prove his creative skills to hotsy-potsy New York ad agency creative directors in hopes of landing a job at their agencies. Not the easiest of tasks, certainly. Even getting an interview with these Madison Avenue mad men is a feat in itself. These CDs are the cream of the crop, the top dogs, the head honchos. Googling their names brings up scores of awards and articles, accolades, and accomplishments. What Googling their names doesn't bring up, however, is a slew of paid ad word spots. Why should they, who Googles the names of top New York ad agency creative directors? I'll tell you who does, the same people that Google your name: you.

Brownstein knew that we all are selfish, egotistical schleps who have, on multiple occasions, all Googled ourselves to see what comes up. And you know what came up when six of the top creative directors in New York Googled themselves? An ad placed by Brownstein for $6, right at the top of the paid Google search. The ad encouraged the CDs to hire Brownstein. Four of the six found his novel approach so engaging, they brought him in for an interview. He received two job offers and now works for one of the top shops in New York. All for $6 and a little novel thinking. /Google

Brownstein's approach proves one important fact about novelty: it's staring us all in the face right now. Brownstein sells creativity, that is his trade, that's his features and benefits. He found a novel way to both say and prove that characteristic to his targeted audience. A monster idea any of us could have grabbed had we seen the potential.

One of the most novel approaches to advertising and marketing is the concept of "character transference." The concept behind character transference is that products aren't advertised at all. Instead, the emotions or character of the brand are offered to the audience with the goal being that the audience will then apply the character they experienced to the brand by way of transference. The audience is more willing to appreciate that brand and transfer that quality for the specific reason that the brand chose to *not* attempt to advertise to them. Admittedly, this level of novelty is often reserved for brands that can afford to unadvertise to their audience and build a brand slowly and organically. This method is most often used in conjunction with traditional methods, almost as a philanthropic exercise but has become increasingly more prevalent as consumers' views of advertising has changed in the last few years.

In 2010, ad agency DDB Stockholm initiated a social experiment for client Volkswagen called "Fun Theory." Volkswagen wanted potential consumers to see their brand as fun, so the experiment aimed to prove that making ordinary things more fun could influence consumers to conciously or subconciously make choices they otherwise wouldn't make. /FunTheory

For instance, if a set of stairs sits idly next to a functioning escalator, what force (other than guilt) would compel people to take the stairs over the escalator? DDB and VW were willing to propose that fun would have an effect on choice. So they promptly turned a Swedish subway staircase into a giant, functioning piano by covering the stairs with sensors that played different notes as you stepped on the piano key-covered staircase. Sure enough, 66 percent more people chose to take the stairs over the escalator. Fun wins. So does novelty.

Or say you're ad agency RPA/Santa Monica and your client, Honda, is willing to take the time to develop the brand character through a little character transference. Honda has always been viewed as an advanced engineering company, so why not try to prove that by creating a branded experience? The result was the Civic Musical Road. /Civic

The engineers cut grooves in a stretch of a Lancaster, California highway at different depths and distances. The grooves in the road cause a noticeable sound in a vehicle that is driving across the road at 55 mph. But not just a noticeable sound, a song. Lancaster, California is in the wide open wild west, so it was only appropriate for the theme song to *The Lone Ranger*, "The William Tell Overture," to be the choice. Hit the highway at 55 mph across this stretch of road and experience advanced engineering for yourself.

Novelty is a powerful tool for marketers and advertisers to use to carry a message to an audience, but novelty alone is insufficient. Like many of the characteristics of monster ideas, originality requires authenticity and an understanding of the character of both the brand and the audience. Too often, marketers and advertisers get fixated on novelty as a medium. The focus should be the product or service, not the novelty. The great ad man Paul Rand once said, "Don't try to be original. Try to be good." But I'd add "try to be novel, too" (don't tell Paul I said that). If you're looking to predict whether your idea has the chance to go monster, one of the questions you'll need to ask is:

Is my idea novel?

MONSTER PARADIGM
NOVELTY

In our Xbox 360 Halo 3 campaign from the introduction, novelty may be harder to find than some of the other characteristics, at least novelty in a sweeping sense. But consider the ways video games are traditionally marketed and the originality in the campaign begins to become apparent. While most games focus on the game itself, often showing scenes from the game in an effort to impress potential game buyers to the depth and detail of the offering, or show video of game play to convey the fun the viewer might have playing the game, the Xbox 360 Halo 3 campaign showed no game play. The strategy behind McCann Worldgroup SF's effort was almost entirely built around the elusive "curiosity factor."

Their goal was clear: create a world of curiosity. Make our audience froth at the mouth with anticipation. So instead of game play videos and action scenes, they left the game environment altogether and did something novel in the game industry: bring the game into real life. They used (fake) real scenarios with (fake) real people reminiscing about (fake) real battles. They not only changed the era to the future, they did so with a realism that blurred the line between what is real and what is fantasy.

Is it novel?

Novelty works best when it encourages
curiosity over memory.

Novelty is an attention device—it brings people to
an idea. It's not the idea itself.

Novelty isn't always about breaking new ground.
Originality can be found in creating new
relationships from familiar experiences.

Novelty can often be found where authenticity
meets opportunity.

The "Spotlight Strategy" marries novelty with product
features or service benefits but must be used carefully.

"Character transference" is unadvertising, the act of
organic brand building through the conveyance of
a brand's character by providing character-driven
experiences with little or no marketing purpose.

Advertising wasn't always the clear-cut path I saw for my career. I graduated with a degree in communication design; at my heart I am a designer. My first job out of college was at a prepress house (raise your hand if you know what film and proofs are. Okay, you two can lower your hands.). The production studio also doubled as a design studio, which was a great first gig for a designer. I learned immediately that concept wasn't everything, we have to be able to execute our ideas. It wasn't long after college that I started my own design firm. We were a full-service shop, which meant we'd design pretty much anything for a buck (not a buck literally, that would be amusingly inexpensive. Two at the very minimum.). I had always found my most joy, though, when I was given the opportunity to solve advertising-related problems. From print ads to TV spots, I loved the creative process in developing both the strategy and the concept, then seeing how that concept could be executed. At one point, I remember thinking, "We should become an ad shop." My partner disagreed. So I killed him (not really. I'm not writing this from prison.). We parted ways when an opportunity to become the creative director at a small ad shop in Costa Mesa, California was presented to me. I'm a big believer in small shops and this particular shop was newly formed from the ownership of the prepress house from which I started my career. Very "full-circle" of me, I know.

Admittedly, I knew little about the advertising industry. I knew I loved the creative process present within it, but I was unfamiliar with the game. Most of my friends despised advertising, like most people at the time I suppose. "Advertising is corporate giants lying to the public to make money," they'd say. They (lovingly) called me the "Manipulation Director," a title I thought was kinda cool. And kinda true. In my professional infancy, I always felt like influencing behavior through advertising was akin to manipulation of sorts. And admittedly, much of my early mind-set in the job furthered that philosophy. That is, until I met Emory.

Emory was an ad guy I ran across in my early career, and he changed the way I looked at advertising. Emory was a brilliant guy, the type of guy that marches to his own beat but you respected him greatly for it. It wasn't long after I first was introduced to him that he had a bit of a nervous breakdown. The sad thing was, I'm not sure he actually had a nervous breakdown, everyone around him just thought he did because that beat to which he was marching took a decisively unusual turn. It was a turn that changed my perspective on the industry, and I'm not alone I'm sure.

Emory started developing ads that were more on the, shall we say, "truthful side" of product communication. Instead of witty headlines that exaggerated key features to make them sound like the most desired feature in the history of mankind, he began presenting the products in their truest light. He got tired of playing the game, he decided people were smart enough to be told the truth about the brands and would flock to them in appreciation. The agency thought he was just being funny, until one of the print ads for their client, Volvo, hit the pubs with the headline "Volvo—They're Boxy But They're Safe." Truthful? Yes. Something Volvo would want to openly say about their automobiles? Evidently not. Before Emory could do any more damage in the agency's mind, a very good friend of his convinced him to take a few weeks off and get some psychiatric therapy.

chasing the monster idea | is it authentic?

The twist with Emory came as he was in the clinic and the numbers started coming in on the Volvo campaign. The numbers came back higher than expected. Much higher. It was one of Volvo's most successful campaign launches ever. It seems Emory was right all along and the agency wanted him back. Emory was always a man of his word, so when he committed to being, well, committed, he had no intention of leaving until his scheduled stay was complete. The agency tried to make do without him, attempting to take a similarly truthful tact with other clients and other ads, but they simply lacked the character Emory had infused. So the agency asked Emory if he would work on other campaigns while in the clinic. He agreed, but with a caveat: that the other clinic "inhabitants" he had befriended and that had befriended him could be involved in the creative process. Which is exactly what happened.

Emory and his group of outside-the-industry collaborators worked on various accounts while in the clinic. For instance, they created print ads for the Greece Tourism Board with the headline "Forget Paris. The French can be annoying. Come to Greece. We're nicer." For luxury car brand Porsche, print ads used the tag line "Porsche. It's a little too small to get laid IN, but you get laid the minute you get out!" While soberingly honest, the ads had a similar effect on the target audience that the Volvo ads provided. The last project Emory worked on while in the clinic was for Japanese technology giant Sony, a TV spot that attempted to find the root of why the electronics maker's products were so superior to American-made competitors'. The spot featured various shots of Sony technicians and engineers designing and producing various products, then ended with the tag line "Sony—because Caucasians are just too damn tall" alluding to the fact that the Japanese culture is generally shorter in stature on average to the American culture, a fact that allows the Japanese engineers to work closer to the electronics and pay more attention to the details. Not exactly the tact most (read: all) advertisers would take to market a company, certainly, but the tact garnered huge results. All monster ideas.

If any of them were true, that is. I'm sure most of you caught on when the Volvo headline was floated, but for those who are unfamiliar with Dudley Moore's fine film career, everything in that story that spoke of Emory was in fact from a 1990 movie called *Crazy People*, starring the aforementioned Dudley Moore as ad exec Emory Leeson and Daryl Hannah as, well, a patient-slash-love interest in the psych ward where Emory was sent. While the second half of that story was obviously fictional, the first half was indeed true. Even the part where I admit that meeting Emory changed my perspective on advertising.

Why can't advertising be less manipulating and be more truthful? The answer is it can, and it has. I would propose, however, that the reason advertising has been more truthful in the last decade isn't a response to a sudden ethical compass or a legislative act. I suspect it has more to do with the Internet and the power the average consumer has to generate backlash than with any lofty change of heart.

The Internet has given a global voice to the consumer, something they simply didn't have before. Before the advent of the Web, if a consumer felt duped or lied to by marketing, their response was limited to just changing their own behavior and perhaps influencing a small group of friends or family. Now, a consumer can go online and post to the view of millions of potential consumers the fallacy of marketing claims. The impact is simply greater, so companies are forced to take a different approach.

Don't get me wrong, I'm not saying all corporate entities are lying weasels that only care about taking your money by any means possible (although I'm sure a few come to mind). I'm just saying the veil of anonymity has been lifted and corporations have to consider the individual in a way they previously could ignore if they desired. This adds another layer to the debate over authenticity in marketing and advertising.

Authenticity in advertising and marketing comes in two distinct flavors: brand authenticity and audience authenticity. Marketing efforts can succeed and fail in one or both attempts. Brand authenticity is being true to the character of the brand, what that brand stands for. Audience authenticity is presenting that message to the audience in a way that treats that audience appropriately to who they are.

Generally speaking, corporate branding is an exercise that works to equate certain desirable characteristics to a company or product. Whether that be security (think Wells Fargo, State Farm), wholesome (think General Mills, Kraft), fun (think Disney, Volkswagen), or convenient (think Betty Crocker, Visa), branding communicates to us what we should feel about the product or service offered. When we talk about brand authenticity, we are talking about advertising or marketing that represents these brand characteristics in a truthful way.

For instance, if you're Disney and you're marketing Disneyland to me as a consumer, I have a brand personality that I immediately assign to the Disney brand. Disney equals fun, it equals fantasy, it equals family. So any attempt to put those characteristics aside and tell me how affordable Disneyland is misrepresents the brand character. I don't know Disneyland to be affordable, I know it to be fun. It feels inauthentic to position Disneyland as an affordable attraction.

Now Disneyland can speak to affordability if it deems it necessary, but to do so authentically would mean using the context of fun or fantasy or family to carry that message. Through the filter of who Disney has built themselves to be to the consumer, messaging will feel far more authentic.

So why is it important to be authentic? Why should we, as advertisers and marketers, care about presenting ourselves authentically through the character of the brand? I'd answer that question by asking another:

How do you feel when you find out you've been lied to?

We've all been lied to at some point in our lives. Someone, somewhere has hurt us by trying to make us believe something that simply wasn't true. Whether that was a child who tried to hide a mistake they made by lying to you about the outcome, or a boss who promised a raise and gave it to another, or a spouse who said they'd taken care of that thing only to find out they didn't and now you're screwed. When we are lied to, we get angry, we get hurt, we get revenge (Okay, that part was just me, but you might relate.). No one likes being lied to and few are willing to trust those who say one thing but do another. The same is true with advertising and marketing.

While we may not be lying about who a brand is to the consumer, choosing to take a path that doesn't fall through the filter of the brand character causes confusion in the marketplace, and it dulls the trust that is being built between brand and consumer. If a brand has constantly communicated to the consumer, "Know this about us over all else—we are good for you" but they spend their marketing and advertising efforts to try and convince the consumer that their convenience is of utmost importance, there are conflicting messages.

As consumers, we're relatively willing to forgive certain characteristics in exchange for others. If you're Disneyland, I'm willing to forgive affordability in exchange for family fun. In short, I'll pay more if the family fun experience is all that they say it is. They don't have to be affordable, their brand character has value that outweighs affordability to me. But if those messages are mixed, I'm uncertain how to view the brand, and what to give up in exchange for what. Each becomes tainted with the other, I no longer feel that there is overwhelming value in either claim.

The cost for brand inauthenticity is often greater than the success of an authentic brand exchange. People come to expect that brands are being truthful with them. When a brand is truthful, it often goes unnoticed. But when a brand is found to be inauthentic, consumers typically react in negative fashion whether that be inactivity or mockery, neither being favorable responses to a marketing or advertising effort.

McDonald's had such an occurrence back in 2005. The fast-food behemoth has done a pretty remarkable job over the years of being completely and totally authentic to their brand character. Their marketing rarely tries to step outside of who they are in an effort to be something they're not. Even in instances when they do, the rest of their marketing machine can usually rescue any wayward efforts so that the public never hears of them. Unfortunately for them, one got out and made a bit of an example out of what happens when authenticity is absent from communication.

The McDonald's dollar menu campaign aimed to bring an extra level of cost-effective food options to their audience. In an effort to become relevant to the young, urban, hip crowd, however, the campaign turned decisively unmonstrous. When corporations try and introduce urban slang into their marketing and advertising, there's rarely a success story to tout, it almost always crashes and burns into a steaming hot bowl of death soup. For McDonald's, the choice to combine the inhabitants of the dollar menu with good-looking, urban youths looking longingly at the affordable menu options is one thing. Choosing to connect the two with the campaign headline, "I'd Hit It" was an entirely different thing. The campaign, in an attempt to prove McDonald's is hip and down with the street lingo, just promoted good-looking, urban youths are interested in having sex with a burger, because that's what "hittin' it" means on the street. Umm . . . oops.

The campaign was pulled when the brass found out they didn't have the street cred they thought. The strategy was fairly sound, McDonald's wanted to appeal to a younger audience so finding places to relate is of utmost importance. The effort was just inauthentic to the brand character of McDonald's. The fast-food chain isn't known to the consumer as urban or hip, it's known as convenient, affordable, and fun. Straying from that brought the inauthentic attempt to the forefront and made the misstep recognizable.

Proof that 2005 was the year of the recorded misstep, usually deft Sony tripped up on a campaign for their Playstation Portable device. In an effort to appeal to what Sony called the "urban nomad," the technology and entertainment company hired local graffiti artists in major metropolitan areas to spray paint cartoon kids playing the device on the sides of buildings and walls in the city. The attempt was to make it more urban art than tagging, but that culture sniffs out corporate intent to seem urban and cool from authentic street art pretty easily.

The outrage came from multiple sides. First, city governments didn't appreciate a blatant disregard for the city's antigraffiti legislation, a fight that would probably be worth it for Sony in the long run if the campaign was successful. But what made the campaign take a turn for the worse was when the street culture the ads were meant to influence saw right through the corporate involvement in their art and began countertagging the ads with anti-Sony sentiments. Probably not what Sony had in mind. The campaign failed on authenticity more so than execution. Sony is known as a technology company, they're stylish, savvy, and techy. The urban relationship, outside of that filter, translated as forced and transparent.

Authenticity takes courage. Courage to know what you are and what you're not. Courage to know who your audience is, what they perceive of you, and how to address that perception. Courage to know where your faults are and address them openly rather than hide them and pretend no one else knows about them. Advertising and marketing has always had the task of playing up the good and downplaying the bad, that's part of the strategy of developing monster ideas, ones that both focus attention on what the company or product does well but also one that addresses how to handle what isn't so great. Success and failure of a campaign or effort often hang on the subtlety of how that is handled. Take, for instance, two competitors who chose to use the same medium at the same time for the same purpose but experienced very different results; one chose an authentic approach, the other handled the authenticity issue with less tact.

In 2007, retail powerhouses Target and Walmart both ventured into the social media space to expand their back-to-school campaigns. The understanding is the audience (students) actively participates in social media sites like Facebook, so it seems a proper medium to reach the audience with a reminder that either carries all their necessary back-to-school supplies. Again, both efforts were part of a larger campaign that touched on both traditional and nontraditional marketing mediums.

Target's Facebook campaign was part of their larger "Hello, Goodbuy" campaign developed by ad agency AKQA. In true Target fashion, the overall campaign was bold and stylish. The Facebook campaign, however, was less so. Instead of their traditional storytelling tactics, the agency chose to alter the strategy for the

Facebook arm of the campaign. The creative director at AKQA, Mauro Cavalletti, reasoned, "Our attitude had to be that we were taking advantage of an environment that already exists; we aren't there so much to tell a story, but to put on a party, giving the students a platform for social interaction."

It's an unusual approach, sell by not selling, but the thought was that in this space, it was more authentic to open conversations than to sell product. Talk first, sell later. Target decided giving consumers a place to interact with their brand in a less salesy way was more appropriate for this medium. Discounts and promotions weren't a part of the Facebook effort, and all links from banner advertising within the Facebook community didn't lead back to the formal Target commerce site, they led back to the fan page that was set up for the campaign.

The fan page wasn't as overtly polished and perfect as you'd expect from a retailer that has developed the brand character of being design savvy because the agency felt that in this space, with this audience, polish is a sign of corporate manipulation. It wasn't in tune with the campaign strategy to use the social media space authentically to both the brand character and the audience. "People expect to see design and polish (from Target's traditional marketing), but on a social network the . . . site has to reflect the visual language of its members," Cavalletti commented. The fan page provided a place for the audience to congregate and talk about Target stores, like which ones had coffee shops or shorter lines. Not all comments were positive, certainly, as you'd expect in a wide-open discussion of a retailer the size and scope of Target, but overall the discussion was authentically driven to be positive surrounding the brand. In short, their decisions to tailor the message to the audience was authentic and accepted as such, a monster idea.

At the same time, Walmart had decided to use the social media site to extend their own back-to-school campaign. Walmart has become a bit of a lightning rod for corporate control as of late. Many people have voiced a distaste for their hiring practices or corporate policies. Unfortunately, in a world as connected as ours, these voices seem to be heard in much greater volume than those who have an affinity for the brand and what it stands for. Walmart has been fighting these voices for years, trying to shake off the stigma attached. Right or wrong, truthful or fabricated, the stigma is still there.

That said, Walmart has always had the brand character of affordability, it has a discount mentality and is known for it's low prices. This brand character has led Walmart to unprecedented success in the marketplace, and they've done a good job promoting that brand character authentically through their traditional marketing vehicles.

Walmart's Facebook effort failed to carry that same authenticity. First, the retailer decided to tailor the messaging of the campaign arm around style, a characteristic that while perhaps true, isn't a part of their brand character. It was a conflicting message with consumers who knew and generally loved Walmart for their affordability. People didn't know them for style, they knew Target for style. They knew Walmart for low prices but the Facebook campaign conflicted with that knowledge.

Second, and probably more damaging, the decision was made not to open the discussion forums feature, instead opting for wall posts as the primary communication vehicle. This sent a loud-and-clear message that Walmart didn't want to open the communication up to receive yet more damning responses. Walmart's fear of backlash led it to close off the communication and create something far more one-sided in an effort to control the conversation. While strategic, the tact simply doesn't play out well on a social network made for open conversation. The result was angry anti-Walmart messages left as wall posts and a general lack of attention to the campaign element.

Walmart's lack of success on the campaign came from the lethal cocktail combo of an inauthentic brand message and an inauthentic audience exchange. Audience authenticity was the greater offense in this case. Being authentic to the audience involves both developing messaging that is appropriate and compelling for the audience as well as developing messengers that are compelling and appropriate to the mediums. The McDonald's example from earlier highlights what happens when the message is contrived and forced to an audience and the Walmart example shows what happens when the medium the audience is using to experience the brand isn't used authentically.

When a brand isn't authentic with it's brand character, it typically leads to confusion. There's usually very little public response to confusion, consumers are rarely angered to the point of backlash if they've been confused by conflicting brand messages. Inauthentic audience representation, however, is often viewed differently. This is where people often feel lied to. When a brand tries to trick or deceive the consumer, and that deception is uncovered, it's not usually a quiet affair. That's why audience authenticity is so prevalent in monster ideas, the ideators developed a way to treat that audience authentically and the audience responded to take the idea monster. The absence of authenticity often results in the exact opposite response.

In 2006, Sony approached guerrilla marketing agency Zipatoni to help them promote their new PSP handheld gaming device. The result: a blog called alliwantforxmasisapsp, set up by a guy who desperately wants a PSP for Christmas. The teenager running the blog spoke often of his desire for a PSP through video and posts, brought in friends that could help him convince his parents to buy him the device for Christmas, even T-shirts that he designed to announce his desires to acquire one. All relatively understandable requests and actions for an Internet savvy teen in America who just wants a killer piece of technology to play with.

If it was true. Turns out, the blog wasn't a blog, it was a "flog," a fake blog completely set up by Sony and the agency to try and go viral with the campaign. They attempted to use poor grammar and misspelling to imply a level of authenticity that simply wasn't there, and the effort was called out almost immediately. The audience for the PSP are incredibly Internet savvy and can sniff out corporate tomfoolery pretty easily, which they did. A simple WHOIS search found the registrar of the domain to be Zipatoni and that was all she wrote. The effort immediately threw up a sail and rode the winds of terribly bad press for both Sony and the agency. Gamers aren't exactly tolerant folks, especially when corporate players in their industry are deceiving them, and they let loose. The campaign has since become the example of what happens when brands are inauthentic with their audience.

The Sony PSP debacle was more a failure of deception than a failure of medium. They used the medium correctly, targeted the right audience but failed to connect authentically to them, and it cost them dearly. The audience inauthenticity had to do with method more than message (although the message wasn't terribly compelling, either).

Monster ideas are born from an authentic brand message being conveyed to an authentic audience in an authentic way.

If the medium of communication doesn't fit that strategy, another should be chosen. As marketers, we often get enamored with medium opportunity, especially in the category of new media. We make the mistake of diving into the pool without a proper understanding of what that pool means to the audience and how to use it authentically for our brand. Sony made the mistake of attempting to force viral, to take it out of the hands of the consumer. General Motors made the mistake of putting it in the hands of the consumer in the first place (proving that there's no one philosophy that is always right, it's entirely brand and audience specific), and unfortunately, appealing to the wrong audience in the process.

In 2006, GM got on the "user-generated content" bandwagon by launching a campaign that allowed Web site visitors the ability to create their own TV spot for their mammoth SUV, the Chevy Tahoe. Visitors could put the spot together from a series of pre-shot clips, adding the ability to overlay whatever text they deemed appropriate for their spot. The finished spots were uploaded to a gallery on the site to give viewers the chance to vote on the most popular variations. Sounds harmless, right? A good way to let those Tahoe enthusiasts and closet creatives have a shot at expressing both their love for the gargantuan vehicle and their previously untapped directorial talents. Give the power to the people.

Unfortunately for GM, the "people" aren't always Tahoe enthusiasts but they are all closet creatives. As a matter of fact, many of the "people" find it considerably more entertaining of a spot if it was used sarcastically or juvenilely to create spots that pasted the Tahoe as earth-destroying, pollution-spewing, Napoleon-complex-stroking, obscenity-inspiring, or worse. Many of the spots painted the Tahoe and GM in a decisively negative light. But they knew that was coming, we knew that was coming. The Target model explored earlier proved that when you give a forum to the masses, you have to have the stomach to swallow inevitable criticism. The question becomes: (a) how much criticism? and (b) from whom?

General Motors commented that they knew negative portrayals were coming, but the negative criticism only represented 20 percent of the overall response. That doesn't seem like much in the grand scheme, right? True, 20 percent of the responses coming back negative isn't a huge number, but remember the purpose for all those spots. They were being uploaded for people to watch and vote for their favorites. Twenty percent isn't a huge number if viewers watched them all and experienced the other 80 percent in contrast. But let's consider why we would watch these videos in the first place. To take the time to watch these user-generated spots, we'd need a level of entertainment that rewarded us for that time. Just watching spot after spot of glowing Chevy Tahoe ads probably isn't compelling enough to warrant our attention. Which would we rather watch, the spot that feels like a spot you'd see on TV or the mockery version that is solely intended to be funny or alarming? Chances are, we'd choose the irreverence over the buttoned-up. We'd probably seek more of the negative spots than the positive spots, because the negative spots are novel variations and we're curious to see what the next person said. So even if 80 percent of the spots were positive, with what brand message do we, as the consumer, leave the experience?

And look at where this brand exchange took place. It occurred on the Web, a place where humor is the rite of passage for viral content and the 15- to 28-year-old prankster resides in earnest. I don't know the demographic of the audience for the Chevy Tahoe, but I'm fairly certain the 17-year-old weberazzi isn't in that group. That's not to say the Web is just a playground of the absurd, it's a viable destination for many marketing and advertising campaign efforts. But the nature of this particular effort is far more tailored to the youthful junior comedian than the serious Chevy Tahoe crowd. The medium and message doesn't fully match the audience.

In their defense, GM stated their intention was to let people share their opinions openly, understanding there would be the opposing forces that naturally show up on any open medium such as the Web and that the buzz generated around the campaign and their willingness to put the brand message in the hands of the audience was worth it in the end. I would venture to say, though, that they would have preferred a more positive reflection.

The inauthentic method to both the Sony and GM campaigns were due in part to a misunderstanding of the audience and what they expect from the mediums they consume. In GM's case, the audience took advantage of GM's poor judgment to provide an open forum to the wrong audience, and that audience made them pay. In Sony's case, consumers felt that the company tried to lie to them, they attempted to deceive the audience to achieve a greater corporate goal. Deception has, unfortunately, been connected to marketing and advertising for decades. It can exist within the fine print of an ad or be prevalent in the core of a campaign. Either way, consumers have become wary of advertising and marketing claims. More trusted sources tend to be given a greater consideration. We'd trust the word of a friend over the claims of an ad any day. That's why the idea of street-level brand evangelism has become such a desired goal for brands.

Brand evangelism is simply the goal of having users or consumers of your brand doing the brand messaging for you. People that have a great experience with a brand or product tell their friends and family about the positive experience, and that leads to a positive view of the product or brand in the eyes of a new consumer. We are often brand evangelists and don't even know it. When we tell a friend about the new Mac we just bought and how great it is or come by to pick them up in the new Jeep Wrangler we just purchased, we're evangelizing. We are spreading the brand message of the company or product for the company or product in a far more authentic way than advertising or marketing alone can ever do. But what happens when even that trust is treaded upon by marketing and advertising?

You get stealth marketing.

Stealth marketing is the practice of purposefully planting brand evangelists in the path of consumers. If the word of our friends or acquaintances we meet are such a powerful force in our views of brands and our buying habits, then brands want to have more evangelists on the ground, even if they have to plant them.

The 2009 film *The Joneses* (where an apparently average family moves into an upper-class neighborhood only to reveal that they are actually planted there by marketing agencies to sell products to their neighbors through the ideology of "keeping up with the Joneses") brings to light the practice of stealth marketing, where people we learn to trust are plants to influence our opinions in a favorable way toward certain brands or products. Sometimes it's simply bringing the product to the consumer in a way, they can experience it firsthand, and sometimes it's a longer con to gain trust on a personal level for the purpose of selling product. Stories of young women in clubs and bars who clandestinely chat up guys and ask them to take their picture with their new camera phone so the consumer can experience the features to stories of couples at resort vacations befriending other couples so they can talk about the great new handbag they bought or the new titanium driver they're using have surfaced over the years as examples of stealth marketing. The practice is intended to gain false trust in order to sell product.

Regardless of your feeling over stealth marketing (some feel it's an effective technique, others feel it's despicable. I tend to lean toward the latter, but that's just me), the harm the technique can do toward a brand if the truth of the messenger ever came to light would be irrevocable. It's one thing to be lied to by advertising or marketing, it's another to be lied to by someone we trust in concert with advertising or marketing. It's the ultimate risk/reward marketing venture. Tread carefully.

While I am presenting authenticity as a quality of monster ideas, it really acts as both a stand-alone quality and a characteristic of the other qualities we've explored. Authentically entertaining, authentically novel, etc. The truth is without authenticity, no other quality has the power to carry an idea into monsterland. As marketers and advertisers, we need to be brutally honest about who we are, what brand character we either have or are perpetrating, who our audience really is, and to what they respond. This honesty will serve as the undercurrent to our monstrous ideas. If you're looking to predict whether your idea has the chance to go monster, one of the questions you'll need to ask is:

Is my idea authentic?

MONSTER PARADIGM
AUTHENTICITY

Taking a peek back at our Microsoft Xbox 360 Halo 3 campaign from the introduction, ad agency McCann Worldgroup SF needed to be very mindful of authenticity in the campaign. So mindful, in fact, that the campaign concept revolves almost exclusively around making the experience more authentic than just a video game could produce alone. The fantasy world the game exists within is meant to provide an escape for gamers, something they can saturate themselves with in a way that puts them right there with the game characters. They are willing to accept this experience as authentic, it's why they play: to make fantasy feel like reality, even for a small period of time. The more authentic the experience, the more accepted the product. The campaign looked to create a world so authentically real, the audience would openly have a tough time telling what was real and what was fantasy. This comes through in every aspect of the campaign, from the human personification of the story characters from within the game to the alternate reality Web experience outside of the game to the diorama created to memorialize the (fake) battle. In this campaign, authenticity reigns.

Is it authentic?

Two types of authenticity: brand authenticity and audience authenticity.

Brand authenticity is the act of being truthful to the brand character or position within the marketplace.

Audience authenticity is the act of understanding the audience, what they expect, and how they consume the media being used.

Inauthentic brand messaging leads to confusion. Inauthentic audience exchange leads to ridicule, backlash, and death (not really death, but close).

Monster ideas are both brand authentic and audience authentic.

Stealth marketing is planting brand evangelists to gain trust in order to sell product. Run away. Fast.

It took only eight minutes to sink.

In the mid-1800s, steamboats owned the river ways of America's burgeoning trade business. These behemoth steamers would carry cargo and passengers across the "new frontier," providing opportunity to entrepreneurs willing to risk the dangers of the open plains. As townships began to emerge along the banks of America's mightiest Midwestern rivers, steamboats acted as conduits connecting homesteaders and settlers with the materials necessary to build a new life. The steamboat *Arabia* was no different, spending most of her time paddling between upstart Kansas City and her sister city on Missouri's eastern border, St. Louis.

On August 30, 1856, an otherwise normal day along the edge of the "Mighty Mo," the steamboat *Arabia*'s days of chugging powerfully down the Missouri River abruptly came to an end. She struck a submerged walnut tree whose roots held strong in the muddy river bed and tore a hole through her hull wide enough to bring the fully stocked steamer to the bottom of the river in eight minutes, leaving just her smokestacks above the surface of the surging river. Everyone aboard, save for a stubborn mule that refused to leave, were able to climb aboard lifeboats and make it to shore. The cargo, however, went down with her.

There have been three separate attempts to reach her over the 150-year period since she went down, two early attempts and one successful last attempt in 1988. The "treasure" hunters embarking on the first two attempts clearly knew the *Arabia* had left port just two hours before she sunk, completely stocked, including what was noted as "400 barrels of Kentucky's finest whiskey," along with 2.5 tons of everything from tools frontiersmen would use to build homes out west to the plates and dishes used to feed them. In between was a nineteenth century Walmart of pre-Civil War era goods, from clothes to food. What the *Arabia* was not carrying, however, was gold. At least, none listed on the official ship's cargo manifest.

Just 21 years after the sinking, two men invested $2,000 toward trying to reach the *Arabia*, a sizable sum considering the enormous effort it would take to reach her and the *Arabia*'s apparently pedestrian cargo. The Missouri River had shifted course so dramatically since the sinking, the men were 50 yards from the waters edge and, according to their calculations, the *Arabia* lay beneath their feet . . . on dry land. The Missouri had no banks, so it often shifted and moved, leaving layers of moist, condensed soil that evolved into fertile farmland. They drilled a small passage down and actually reached the deck of the *Arabia*, only to bring up a barrel of hats. Discouraged and convinced that the *Arabia* wouldn't offer more than trinkets, they abandoned their attempt, as their "treasure" lay in the hopes of finding even one of the 400 barrels of Kentucky's finest. In the late 1800s, 20-year-old whiskey was sure to fetch a king's ransom on the open market, but instead of ransom they found wet leather when they were looking for liquid gold. But were they? As was customary with unorthodox government requests at the time, the county clerk who approved the excavation sent his apprentice to monitor the dig. A strange scribbled entry in the apprentice's ledger, the last notation of a list titled "Intended Cargo Recovery" reads "McCoy's dowry." This single anomaly is the only item listed in the apprentice's ledger but not listed on the ship's official cargo manifest.

John Calvin McCoy, known as the "Father of Kansas City," owned a trading post in Westport Landing, where the *Arabia* would have docked to load its cargo. McCoy's post just so happened to be the last point of contact for both travelers crossing the California, Santa Fe, and Oregon trails west and native American Indian tribes indigenous to the region. Folklore in the area talks about a dowry McCoy inherited from his Native American bride, a bride rarely seen. It was always assumed McCoy had managed a deal with the local Wyandot tribes to allow him to continue running the trading post "uninhibited," a deal that would be mutually beneficial to both the tribe and McCoy. The tribe would have handshake access to tools, clothing, and weapons in exchange for the beautiful daughter of one of the tribe's elders . . . and the dowry of Native American gold that customarily accompanied such a union.

Along with the inherent dangers with our nation's push for westward expansion, this was also an unsettled time in our nation's history. Union and Confederate ranks were beginning to divide the country as it seemed we were destined for civil war. As civil unrest began to spring up in the Kansas City area, and the North/South line was drawn right down the Mighty Mo, McCoy knew the growing Confederate Army across the river would be coming for this infamous but mysterious dowry. When McCoy and his outpost were torched by crusading abolitionists, the dowry was never found. Some believed he hid the dowry in a few of the 400 barrels of Kentucky's finest whiskey that he sent on the *Arabia* that fateful day, five days before the sacking of McCoy's post. It seems the 400 barrels were the only official cargo mysteriously missing from the boat when it was excavated in 1988. Most believe the dowry a fairytale and the barrels lost to the Missouri when the *Arabia*'s hull was breached by

that disastrous snag, but the notation in the apprentice's ledger has only served to fuel the fire. If the barrels weren't on the boat, and McCoy DID hide his dowry in the barrels, he would have ensured he could collect his treasure after the ensuing war. Which can only mean one thing: they're still in Kansas City.

No, that's not the plot of the next box office B movie flop starring the half brother of one of the Baldwin's second cousins, it's the basis for an alternate reality game intended to be an arm of a larger campaign pitch we at Reign were making to the Kansas City Tourism Bureau. The overarching campaign concept revolved around the tag line "You Never Know What You'll Find in KC" and was intended to bring to life the rich historical attributes of the "Paris of the Midwest." The game was meant to engage tourists in the historical undercurrent of the city, allowing them to experience these landmarks in a more encompassing way, as part of a larger fabric that makes Kansas City what it is today. This narrative was only the genesis of a hunt that would take them to prominent city markers and places of interest in a quest to find McCoy's dowry. Through this quest, they would get to experience the city in a novel way, learning about the region and enjoying every minute of their curious, story-driven exploration. Bits and pieces of the story are true (the steamboat *Arabia*'s untimely demise, for instance) but the rest was a tightly woven fabric of fiction and fantasy with a few straggling threads of truth to keep the story from going off the rails entirely. And no, that wasn't John McCoy or actual barrels of 150-year-old Kentucky's finest. Move along, these are not the droids you're looking for.

Story is as old as time. Humans have used stories to pass down history, teach, warn, entertain, and inspire. Historically speaking, we've discovered the earliest forms of communication between people use imagery to depict stories of events or processes. Biblically speaking, Jesus himself used stories, called parables, to communicate the application of Biblical truth. Stories teach us what we should do, how we should act, or where we should go. They warn us of danger, providing examples of what may happen when certain conditions or situations arise. They connect to us emotionally, giving us application to abstract concepts. We are moved through story, we construct the very idea of our lives in the form of a story.

> "Evidence strongly suggests that humans in all cultures come to cast their own identity in some sort of narrative form. We are inveterate storytellers."
>
> —Owen Flanagan
> *Leading Consciousness Researcher*
> *Duke University*

Perhaps most important for marketers and advertisers, though, is that story offers a method to engage consumers with brand characteristics and qualities that are applied and embedded through the context of story.

Stories can be told linearly or nonlinearly. Linear narratives take us on a chronological journey through the story, it has a beginning, a middle, and an end. Nonlinear narratives jump around the story, revealing parts of it along the way but out of chronological order.

The simplest way for me to describe the difference is in the form of pop culture references (due to my obvious lack of literary education and short attention span. Clearly.), so let's think in cinematic form (who doesn't love the movies? Put your hand down, who asked you.). Most narratives are in chronological form, like say the story depicted in the award-winning 1994 film *Shawshank Redemption*. A crime was committed (or not committed), the offending party was put in prison for his crime (or not crime), he developed relationships while in prison, he escaped prison, his friend was released from prison, and they were reunited. A beginning, middle, and end.

A nonlinear story mixes up how that story is told. While the events may or may not happen in chronological order, the telling of that story occurs disjointed or out-of-order. Think of something like the also award-winning 1994 film *Pulp Fiction*, (evidently, I'm obsessed with 1994), which has multiple storylines that are occurring simultaneously, and we're presented each of the storylines at differing points of the narrative. The story works because of a few characters and plotlines that carry through each of the stories, bringing them together in the end (at least what is the end to us as the viewers).

While this book isn't intended to be an exploration of story in mid-'90s American cinematic culture, story plays a significant role in the development of monster ideas. In every monster idea we've examined in this book, there are primary elements of story present because story is the "sticky" quality to each of the campaigns (thank you Malcolm Gladwell and your book *The Tipping Point* for the term "sticky" in reference to an idea's ability to remain relevant and worthy of attention. You officially rock. Carry on.).

In their book *Made to Stick*, Chip and Dan Heath pinpoint story as one of the six primary characteristics ideas need to have to "stick." As they put it:

> A story is powerful because it provides the context missing from abstract prose. This is the role that stories play—putting knowledge into a framework that is more lifelike, more true to our day-to-day existence. Stories are almost always concrete. Most of them have emotional and unexpected elements. The hardest part of using stories effectively is making sure they're simple—that they reflect your core message. It's not enough to tell a great story; the story has to reflect your agenda.

Notice that according to Chip and Dan Heath, story itself contains many of the characteristics we've been discussing about monster ideas: authentic, emotional, and novel. And like most of these characteristics, that last line points to relevance within our storytelling being a factor in the story's ability to carry our brand message to the consumer. It's not enough to tell a great story, the story must be relevant to the emotion or character of the brand or experience. Without this relevance, the story teaches nothing and we, as humans, are constantly looking for order and lesson from the stories we consume.

When we talk about developing a good story for our brand, we can learn a ton from what makes a good story—period. (No, a period doesn't make for a good story, although the absence of a period would probably result a bad one.) A great story is a great story, regardless of whether its intent is to convey a brand's character or inform of a product's ability. For the purposes of our exploration here, we'll define the constructs of a good story as containing these six qualities or considerations:

- A well-defined, singular theme
- Clear characterization
- A well-developed plot
- Stylistically vivid
- Dramatically told
- Audience appropriate

If we take one of our cinematic examples from earlier, *Shawshank Redemption*, we can apply these six qualities to it fairly easily. The theme is clearly hope and redemption, it's even included in the title of the film. The main characters are easily "bucketed" (Andy is the protagonist, he's the hero. We learn to have feelings for him because he's a dreamer and meant to be relatable. Red is the trusted friend, he's mysterious but trustworthy, becomes loyal and compassionate. Warden Norton is the antagonist, he's the villain. Andy's triumph over his heavy hand is part of the redemption), we know what the character's roles are in the story but we get to grow with them through the film. The plot is tight and provides closure through an all-encompassing redemptive ending (strengthening the theme), the 1940s prison setting is shot with a desaturation of color, making the scenes that occur outside the walls of the prison seem that much more vibrant and speaks to the drab, haunting spirit of prison life. The buildup to Andy's escape and how all the pieces of the story leading up to that redemptive moment played a part in that escape adds a wealth of natural drama and heightened climax, and the audience of both film enthusiasts and entertainment seekers are rewarded through the telling of a beautiful story. Each of the qualities of a good story are represented in the film.

I know what you're saying, though. "We're not making movies, we're marketing." I hear you (not really, you said it kinda quiet. Plus, I'm more than likely far away from you right now. Unless you're Brady at the letterpress shop downstairs, but I doubt you're reading this.). In the same way that storytellers develop stories for film, we can develop stories for marketing and advertising, if we're willing to use the same formula. Monster ideas capture the imagination of the audience primarily because they connect with them on an emotional level (plus all the other reasons in this book) and to do that, they have to tell a compelling story. If our idea doesn't tell a compelling narrative, we stand little chance of inspiring any action. The better the story, the better the chance we have at developing a monster idea (see Monster Paradigm: Story at the end of this chapter).

Story in marketing and advertising can and has come in different variations. Some tell the story of one moment in time, some are snippets of larger implied stories, others tell a much larger story, stretching that story across mediums and through experiences. Some stories are completely told within the 30 to 90 seconds of a TV spot, while others use branded content and month-long, real-world experiences to craft an intricate story of brand character. Monster ideas don't follow one repeatable form of story but they do all use story in one way or another to get into our psyche, under our subconscious, and effect us both emotionally and memorably.

Marketers and advertisers often turn to ad agency Chiat/Day's seminal "1984" Apple spot introducing the Mac to the world as the quintessential story-driven marketing effort. Directed by famed film director Ridley Scott, the spot features a fit and trimmed young woman sprinting through what appears to be a factory or environment of mindless minions, controlled by what pulls immediate comparisons to "Big Brother" in George Orwell's classic 1984. The idea being that this heroine is coming to free the world of conformity and control by Big Brother, referring to the proliferation of PC computers. The woman arrives at a giant screen where the Big Brother character is speaking to the minions and she throws a sledgehammer at the screen to destroy it. The spot is widely considered a watershed event in advertising and one of the most successful spots of all time. /1984

The computer, the Mac, is never shown (outside of a cameo appearance as an abstract image on the white tank top the heroine dons), but the message is clear. Whatever this is (curiosity), it's going to revolutionize how we think about computing. The story engrained this, it assigned this feeling, this brand character without having to say it. Within the construct of story, it proved it instead.

Television spots have been marketing's medium-of-choice for story, as the cinematic potential provides fertile storytelling ground. That's not to say that a monster idea incorporating story can only exist in video, storytelling isn't reserved for television. A great story can be told through any medium, but video has certainly presented compelling stories that have turned monster. We've all experienced and remembered the 30- to 90-second stories from brands like Jell-O (think Bill Cosby), the Budweiser Frogs, Joe Isuzu's incessant lying, the comparison of fried eggs and our brain on drugs, the never-ending travels of the Energizer Bunny, that crotchety old lady inquiring politely about the Lilliputian size of her hamburger patty, the battle between tastes great and less filling, and a picky little boy who really liked a bowl of Life cereal. We remember them because they all took us for a 30- to 90-second story ride, equated the character of the brand with the story line, and told us how to feel about the brand.

/PowerfulStuff

Other small scale, 30- to 90-second monster ideas have yet to garner the historical accolade that accompany that previous list, but have used story to grow monstrous in the short time they've had with the consumer. One such story is the one told for Virgin Media produced by agency RKCR/Y&R titled "Powerful Stuff" in 2010. The 90-second TV spot follows a young man onto a subway car as he sits across from a businessman and takes out his Virgin mobile device. He clicks on the device and the subway car transforms to a café and the businessman transforms to a beautiful woman smiling shyly back at him. Another click drops two buddies in the seats next to him and the car transforms into a buzzing concert scene. From the club atmosphere, we're taken to the subway car as a movie theater, that same beautiful girl snuggling next to him in the theater seat. We're immediately transformed into a transport ship for a group of futuristic video game soldiers, our hero sitting shoulder to shoulder as the ship docks and the soldiers run forcefully out into the light of the bay doors. As he steps off the ship, we're taken back to the subway station where instead of the ship he is leaving, we see it to be the subway car as he arrives at his destination. A glance up finds the same girl from the subway car shyly smiling at him as she steps onto the car. The tag line appears: "A World of Entertainment on Your Virgin Mobile." Just one in a series of similar stories produced as TV spots, Virgin has enjoyed its highest level of subscriptions and highest customer spend rate during the time the campaign has run.

/Fate

We've come to expect compelling stories from certain brands. It's hard to imagine, for instance, a brand experience from Nike without a gripping narrative, regardless of medium. Nike agency Wieden + Kennedy has developed a connection with athletes and consumers that almost requires a deep, rich story with every effort, and they've yet to disappoint. In 2009, one such award-winning effort was called "Fate" and it chronicled the lifelong journeys of NFL stars running back LaDainian Tomlinson and strong safety Troy Polamalu. The parallel story begins with both of them as youngsters, engaging in the things that youngsters do, from a baby kicking on an ultrasound image to running away from dad with a head full of shampoo. In separate scenes, a child version of Tomlinson is seen running down a hall, stealthily weaving between pillars while Polamalu is seen jumping from the couch to the coffee table (completely destroying the table) and running full steam into a pile of bean bags. The scenes progress as the two get older, mixing in scenes of Pop Warner football and running through the sprinklers. Tomlinson is shown in high school riding his bike swiftly to football practice while Polamalu runs over fools on the basketball court. The progression leads to college, with scenes of both in their college uniforms coming out of the tunnel are shown, then training shots of Tomlinson running through dummy tacklers and Polamalu running stadium stairs in the snow. The climax of the spot is a game in which Tomlinson's team, the Chargers, are playing Polamalu's team, the Steelers. Tomlinson gets the ball and starts around the outside as Polamalu chases to meet him at the line. The two collide as they fall to the ground, popping up and slapping each other on the helmet in congratulations of a good play. The end card, "Leave Nothing" is displayed with the Nike logo.

In true Nike fashion, a specific product isn't shown. Nike has always felt that story and brand character trickles down to all of their products. If consumers believe Nike understands them, understands their goals and desires and fears, then each of their products inherit those qualities naturally. Nike markets to the 18- to 34-year-old in all of us, a philosophy that transcends shoes or shirts or gear. Story provides the realm to take us on that journey.

Aside from TV, the Web has opened up an entirely different avenue for story. Narratives that use the Web as their medium can be told without the constraints of time or regulation, they can be told with an infinite world of interaction and information, the marriage of entertainment and education. For instance, the Web has revealed a new medium marketers can use to tell a more compelling story than TV can provide: long-form branded content. Because time isn't a limitation, marketers can create fully developed mini-stories that develop and reveal brand character in a more saturating way. If it's entertaining and compelling, the brand's character can be embedded into the story and be communicated to the audience willingly.

We explored an example of long-form branded content in the chapter on entertainment when we examined the BMW Films campaign "The Hire." These 10-minute short stories didn't end with a "Buy a BMW" message, and they didn't list the features of the luxury automobile. The stories embedded the features of the car in the context of the story. As "The Driver" would enter his car or get involved in a chase scene, the camera would catch a particular feature or styling of the car in the frame but more so than that, the idea was to equate "cool" with BMW. The audience would be engaged with the story and receive a branded BMW message at the same time.

/TheHire   /JohnnieWalker

Another example of long-form branded content is the monster idea BBH/London developed for Johnnie Walker in 2009 called "The Man Who Walked Around The World." The agency saw an opportunity to use the Web to distribute a long-form ad telling the naturally compelling story of Johnnie Walker himself, from his humble grocer beginnings to the brand it is today. The story, by itself, is almost enough. But add to that a well-crafted form of delivery, and the story comes to life in a way that peaks our curiosity and compels us to know more. The five-and-a-half minute video, shot on a winding path on a rocky hillside in Perthshire Scotland, stars Scottish actor Robert Carlyle of *The Full Monty* and *Transpotting* fame. The actor walks along this dirt path past a bagpiper, who he tells to "shut it" to begin the spot. The camera stays directly in front of the walking actor as he begins the story of the long walk John Walker began in the 1800s when he started distilling the now famous spirit.

Two things jump out at you immediately about the story. First, the entire five-and-a-half minutes of the spot are shot in one take. There are no cutaways or editing, Carlyle tells the entire story, beginning to end, in one take which makes the spot feel far more epic as he is able to tell the story from memory, with all the inflection and drama necessary to draw the viewer in. Second, as Carlyle is telling the story, he's passing staged props along the road that he interacts with or adds visual flavor to the story, so he has to be right on the entire way. As he talks about John Walker opening a grocery store, he walks through a door on the roadway with "John Walker, Grocer" written on the glass of the door. He passes barrels of malt when a part of the story refers to barrels and grabs an example of the signature square bottle from a bar table set along the side of the road right when he is referring to the bottle shape. It's these manual props and the timing of their exchange that makes the story so powerful. This is the novel delivery that took the spot from good to monster.

/TheCube

Monster stories aren't all as simple as a 30-second TV spot or a long-form Web video. There are instances when the story is simple but the delivery requires large-scale methods to authentically communicate the brand character. Ad agency BBDO created such an event to celebrate client HBO's brand character of innovative storytelling. In the ultimate "show, don't just tell" campaign, BBDO with HBO developed a multiplatform campaign called "It's More Than You Imagine." One arm of the campaign aimed to this innovative storytelling technique by creating a series of installations set in three major metropolitan areas. The installations were called "The Cube," dubbed a first-of-its-kind outdoor event. A 14 x 14 cube was constructed in each of the major metropolitan areas, a cube that appeared as a simple HBO-branded giant black box during the day, but at night, the show would start. On each side of the cube was an angle of the same story, a story that was shot at four different angles simultaneously, with each side giving the viewers a different perspective of the story, the characters, and the plot. The only way to fully understand the story was to see it from all four sides.

Two different films were shown, one called *The Heist* and one called *The Affair*, both providing a compelling, multiperspective storyline. For instance, in *The Affair*, the setting was a multiroom home or apartment. There were four characters, a husband, a wife, a maid, and a lover. All four characters are in the house simultaneously, and there's clearly an affair going on but until you see the story from all four sides, revealing character hiding places and near-contact experiences, there's no telling who is having an affair with whom.

Both stories and installations bring the experience of what HBO offers in a brand experience to the audience in an entertaining and novel way. The experience never says "Sign up for HBO," it never has to be that blunt. The story proves the storytelling chops of HBO in a way no traditional ad or marketing effort could ever do.

At the beginning of this chapter, I told you a story that was the basis for an alternate reality game for a pitch to the Kansas City Tourism Board. Alternate Reality Gaming, or ARG for short, is the technique of bringing brand character and interaction into the real world through a live-action game. It weaves fantasy and reality together to allow consumers to immerse themselves in the story of the brand. We most often see ARG executions in the context of cinematic releases, as the natural storylines of a movie make for immersive experiences when pulled off the screen and brought into the realm of reality. ARG offers a form of storytelling that doesn't just take the consumer with them along the story, it allows them to be a part of the story.

For example, when German luxury car maker Audi brought the first A3 model to America, they hired ad agency McKinney to help them launch the model in a memorable way. The agency developed an alternate reality game that was intended to bring a spy movie to life by seeding that the prototype of the car had been stolen. "The Art of the Heist" campaign started with a live theft of the car from the Audi dealership on Park Avenue. Security cameras caught two men smash the window and steal the car. Had someone been driving by the dealership at that exact moment, they would have seen the two men actually smash the window and take the car. Only Audi and the creators of the game knew it was staged. To the world, this was real. /Audi

The next day, at the New York Auto Show, instead of seeing America's first A3, a sign was in the car's place announcing the heist and asking the public for leads. Bloggers from around the world were retelling the story of the missing A3, convinced the act was, in fact, real. Billboards, newspaper ads, and other postings followed, all asking for the public's help in finding the missing A3. A little online investigation would lead folks to the story that Audi had contracted a small, mysterious, high-end art recovery agency to find the missing vehicle. The key employees of this agency could be investigated further to discover strange relationships and murky pasts. The legitimacy of the agency could be corroborated by noticing months of real-world ads placed in art magazines for the firm, reinforcing that this was all legit.

More investigation uncovers a video game designer named Virgil has also offered his services to Audi help find the missing car. Virgil offers his services for free in exchange for Audi's permission to use the cars in his video games. Virgil even shows up at massive video game conventions, being interviewed by reputable publications, all to further the reality of the heist. A blogger named Todd had been keeping track of the entire story so viewers could catch up wherever they dropped into the story. Participants that uncovered and solved coded messages in job postings listed on Web job boards were rewarded with invitations to live events that acted as cover for the retrieval agency. They'd interact with the attendees of the event and ask them to perform clandestine missions for them to help uncover the location of the missing A3.

Other ARG events have created monster buzz for brands, typically around product launches and release dates. Microsoft ran an alternate reality game around the 2001 release of Steven Spielberg's film *Artificial Intelligence: AI*, called "The Beast." The game takes place 50 years after the events chronicled in the film. The game took place mostly online, as misinformation was a key component to the game. It brought to life the characters and places revealed in the film, bringing into real-life that which was complete fantasy, furthering the story to interested players.

Volvo had a similar notion when they sponsored the release of Disney's *Pirate's of the Caribbean: Dead Man's Chest* with an ARG that sent willing hunters in search of a Volvo SUV filled with gold and buried somewhere in the world. The effort drew 52,000 players from the United States alone. So successful was the first game that Volvo followed it up with another ARG for the third installment of the film franchise, *Pirate's of the Caribbean: At World's End*, with a small twist: players knew that this time, it was a chest of gold they were looking for and it was sitting on the bottom of the ocean somewhere. (As a complete side note, the most entertaining part of the entire second Volvo ARG was when the game had to be suspended toward the end when the official treasure-hunting company hired to place the treasure actually *found* real treasure at a nearby shipwreck and had to stop the game to recover it. Oops.)

We are all moved by story. Stories that make us laugh, make us cry, inspire us and scare us, we are all innately storytellers and storylisteners. Jim Loehr, in his book *The Power of Story* says "Stories make sense of chaos; they organize our many divergent experiences into a coherent thread; they shape our entire reality." Story expert and author of the popular *Storytelling Power* blog, Chris King, puts it in plain terms when she says, "A good story is one that touches people in some way. As storytellers, our mission is to involve the audience, make them interact with us and the story, even if it is just in their thoughts or core. A really good story has a sense of truth and resonates with some basic universal aspects of being human." This is especially true of story as a characteristic in monster ideas. Our ability to inspire interaction with our audience is a primary leader to that audience viewing our brand in the way we want them to view it and ultimately engaging themselves in a buy behavior with the product. If you're looking to predict whether your idea has the chance to go monster, one of the questions you'll need to ask is:

Does my idea tell a story?

MONSTER PARADIGM
STORY

Let's look at our own interchapter, nonlinear example of the Microsoft Xbox 360 Halo 3 campaign we introduced in the intro (nonlinear because we reveal bits and pieces of the campaign's story in each chapter, no one revelation more chronologically accurate than the next). The campaign, if nothing else, is completely story-driven, telling the story using a nonlinear method of flashbacks to recount the tale of Master Chief and the battle he, and they, encountered. The more detailed the varying pieces of the campaign are, the more real they seem. The character of the brand is conveyed through this fantasy/reality blur, but the only way to seize the emotion of the consumer is to do it through the context of the story. Without story, the game has no entertainment purpose, there's nothing to accomplish, nothing to overcome. What makes the game popular to the audience is the story the players get an opportunity to immerse themselves within.

If we look at the story that the campaign develops, we can see each of our six story qualities. The theme of "Believe" is the campaign focus, it's a call for participants to believe Master Chief can lead the human race to victory despite overwhelming odds. The character of Master Chief as the ultimate leader is portrayed through the devotion and reverence of the soldiers he led. The plot was created within the game, the campaign developers simply pulled it out and put a face to it in the form of real accounts to the battle.

The vivid nature comes in the form of memories and accounts. In one video, a former soldier under Master Chief is recounting a night that his platoon was secretly bunkered down in a valley in the darkness waiting for Master Chief to rendezvous with them in the morning, while the enemy hunted them all night. He describes the frightening, life-and-death encounter from the actual spot it supposedly took place (years and years later, of course). As he stands at the spot where this occurred, lights hang from trees nearby and as he tells the story of the night to the documentary film crew, he's visibly feeling some of the same fear he supposedly felt that night. As he describes the darkness to the film crew, the director asks if they can turn the lights off to reenact the darkness. He continues the account but this time, he does it at a whisper, naturally quieting as he remembers the emotions he felt that night hiding in the darkness with the enemy nearby.

The campaign creates drama as the toll and enormity of the battle is inserted into a game that is void of both, giving consequence where there was none previously. The campaign is made for the audience who would purchase the game, and the same emotions and anticipation they naturally have for the game's launch is amped through the realism displayed in the campaign. All in all, an extremely well-crafted, nonlinear narrative meant to ultimately sell a video game through the carrier of story.

Does it tell a story?

We, as humans, are innately drawn to story.
It teaches, warns, entertains, and inspires.

Good stories exhibit these six qualities:

- A well-defined, singular theme
- Clear characterization
- A well-developed plot
- Stylistically vivid
- Dramatically told
- Audience appropriate

Stories can be linear or nonlinear.

Transmedia storytelling spans across multiple
mediums to tell a compelling story.

Long-form branded content communicates the
character of a brand through a story.

Alternate reality gaming blurs the line between fantasy
and reality by bringing the story to the audience.

This is the green chapter. Why is it the green chapter, you ask? (If you didn't ask that, try it . . . it's fun.) It's the green chapter because it's different, it's bold, it's going to touch on a subject we don't typically want to consider, it's going to address a "feeling" about our idea more than a quality we may be able to identify. This chapter is the green chapter because it's going to take a chance. It's going to risk failure focusing on something we, as advertisers and marketers, talk a lot about but rarely practice. It's something we preach from the conference table tops to our clients but would find difficult dealing with ourselves. It's going to address a hypocrisy that is at the heart of why some ideas go monster and others shrivel and die, or worse, do nothing. This is the green chapter because green is hulking, green is dangerous, green is unsettling. We're not talking environmentally friendly save-the-earth green, we're talking lean-mean-green-machine green. We're talkin' scaly, growling, monster green. There's no safety in this green, there's no assurance with this green. Green means something is moving and we need to act. Green means all is not necessarily well. It doesn't always mean "bad," but it does always mean "look out." Green is uneasy, like an upset stomach, which is exactly what we need to discuss in terms of our ideas. Why is it the green chapter, you ask?

Because green is scary. And scary is good.

In late 2009, my agency was invited to pitch a client. As I've chronicled earlier, we have a small shop, and this client would be a significant account to win, the type of account that changes the makeup of a shop. It was right in line with the type of clients we had been targeting. They were, frankly, at the top end of the wish list, an opportunity every young shop would dream of getting. The opportunity came early in our timeline, definitely the most public and appealing an opportunity as we had ever had to date. This was very big to us, and we treated it as such.

The pitch was open-ended in that the client asked to see as much as we were willing to show of our idea. As a young agency, we were prone to overpitching like many young agencies do (I think we still are, we so love the pitch process, it's hard to hold back.). We brainstormed, we strategized (is that a real word?), we comped and mocked and shot and cut and wrote and estimated. The resulting campaign was, well, monster. At least we felt like it could be. It had all the hallmarks of a monster idea as we've identified them here. It confronted emotionally, it was authentic to the audience, it created real brand experience, we believed it to be overtly entertaining, it was based on a great brand story and it was certainly novel, especially in the industry. We thought it had a chance to be a monster idea, but in the back of our minds we couldn't shake the truth and we really struggled to weigh client comfort and monster idea potential:

The concept scared us.

The idea was on point, the brand character was legitimate and the stated goals were addressed, but the reality was it didn't "feel" like advertising. It was bold, brash, and in the industry, completely novel. It took some big risks, which was both exhilarating as a creative and horror movie frightening at the same time. We believed in the idea wholeheartedly, we believed it was the right direction, but we also knew this wasn't a headline and pretty picture, we weren't showing the product and listing the features, which was exactly the world they came from. This was going to be polarizing, and we admittedly kept asking ourselves the same question over and over:

Is it right?

Swallowing hard, we believed it was. So we marched into their office on a Friday afternoon and pitched this idea with as much passion and fervor as we could muster. We had to tell the story of what this would do for the brand, what the perception would become and how it would filter to the rest of the product line. We had to sell because we knew if we were scared about the idea, they were certainly going to be as well. We couldn't make them any promises, so we felt we needed to make them visionaries. If we could lay out the monster potential in the idea, they would be able to see both the originality of the concept and the novelty of the delivery and get on board.

The pitch went as well as we hoped it could go. They were engaged and responsive, participated in the freeflowing discussion of possibilities, and even began circumventing possible future obstacles for us. They smiled at the right areas, shook their head in disbelief in others, shared concerned glances and fragile smirks at one another when controversial aspects of the campaign were revealed. All in all, everything we had hoped for. Now the waiting game began. They took a few weeks longer to respond than originally indicated, which was like waiting around for news that your puppy has died—

excruciating. The longer we waited, the more we began to regret the direction we chose. Maybe it was too far, too fast? Maybe they looked it over and thought "are you kidding? We can't do that, it doesn't even say how unique our technology is!" Maybe the unusual delivery methods were just too different than what they were used to. Maybe, maybe, maybe.

The e-mail finally came, and it was neither as bad as we were expecting nor as good as we were hoping. We were neither chosen nor discarded. They wanted to see more. Not more as in "more of what we see here," but more as in "more of how this could be more buckled down." They recognized the concept but felt it was just too wide, it wasn't tight enough. We could understand, it was conceptually broad and a huge departure from what they had been doing (and succeeding at) for years. We were both relieved that we were still in the hunt but bummed that there was more work to do. Then came the decision that forever changed not only that pitch, but how I would approach advertising and marketing for the rest of my career:

I compromised.

As the creative director in a small ad shop, it was my call what we did from there, and I made a bad call. A very bad call that cost us the account.

Because I was scared.

I was scared that the direction was *too* novel, it was *too* entertaining, it was *too* emotional. I was scared that we went too far, and I wanted them to know we could read between the lines of their requests to see that even though they said they liked the concept, that they said they understood and appreciated the novelty, that they said they just wanted to see how it could be dialed down just a touch, that we were smart enough to see that they were uncomfortable with the direction and preferred something just one step further than what they were already doing. So I compromised because I was scared.

We developed a new campaign that didn't just dial it back, it tossed it aside entirely. We developed a campaign that was just a glorified version of what they were already doing. It wasn't novel, it wasn't entertaining, it wasn't story driven. It just was. None of us liked it nearly as much as the first campaign, we all tried to talk ourselves into believing it was just as good but one notch down in the creative department. The only thing we felt strongly about the new campaign was comfort. We were comfortable with the direction. It didn't polarize anything, there was little to disagree with, it was inarguable. It was good, don't get me wrong. It was a good campaign. But that was all it was—good.

We pitched this new campaign a few weeks later. Instead of just the four people on the client side of the table from the first pitch, those four were accompanied by three more, anxiously awaiting what magic we would bring this time around. We pitched the second campaign, but the energy was decisively different. No smiles, no laughter, no concerned glances and fragile smirks shared. They didn't ask the right questions of the campaign when we were finished, the questions that indicate they are trying to figure out how to make it real in their world, they didn't engage in possibilities. They simply thanked us for our time and we left.

Everyone who has ever pitched an idea knows the feeling of possibility and the feeling of failure in a pitch. Some reactions are unmistakable "You guys nailed it" and some reactions are "Thanks, but we didn't like it at all." On the way down the elevator, the latter was thick in the air. We didn't need the e-mail that came a few days later to tell us we didn't win the account, we already knew. But the e-mail provided the motivation I needed to change my perspective on ideation. It gave me the one line that altered my perspective on fear, failure, and marketing. It spoke to me stronger than seven words from a client (or potential client) has ever spoken and changed my philosophy on the business of creativity:

"We didn't think it was creative enough."

I should thank them, really. I'm one of only two people who knows what it felt like when Mola Ram ripped the still-beating heart out of the human sacrifice in *Indiana Jones and the Temple of Doom*. Me and that guy who got lowered into the lava, we're the only ones. I got scared and it caused me to compromise what I knew was right, what I knew had a chance to turn monstrous. I stopped creating for the industry and the brand and started creating for the implied perspective of the client and my fear. I made the single greatest mistake I could make in the development of an idea: I was afraid to fail.

Fear is a completely subjective emotion. What scares some may not scare others. Heights does nothing for me (I'm 6'8" tall, if I was afraid of heights I'd fall down just walking to the bathroom), but others have a debilitating fear of heights. We all fear something, it's the subject and degree that is subjective. Failure is one of those things that most people fear, no one wants to fail, but the degree of fear differs from person to person and creative to creative. But regardless of the line you choose to draw, one thing is a fact: it's not failure we fear, it's the consequences of failure that truly scare us.

If there were no consequences to failure, we'd choose to fail all the time. If jumping off a building to see if we could fly didn't come with the messy splat sound at the bottom and the sharp, sudden pain that accompanies, we'd jump off buildings all the time. We'd never need to weigh decisions, we'd simply act. But consequences are real, so fear of failure becomes real, too. The harsher the consequences, the greater the fear.

Remember back to school, when your teacher would remove the consequence from an assignment to get you to try something new. When that consequence is gone, we're willing to step out of the norm and experiment because there's no reason not to. Put the consequence back, and we'll return to whatever tried-and-true method we can use to make sure we don't fail. When we were kids, success was accomplishing something new. We'd run home to mom to tell her we walked across the monkey bars or did a wheelie. As we got older, success wasn't defined by what we accomplished, but by what we didn't not accomplish (head hurt yet?). Success became the absence of failure rather than the presence of innovation.

Advertising and marketing is one of those industries that has made a living defining success as the absence of failure. We, as advertisers and marketers, would rather take a path that can't be very wrong than a path that could be very right. There's no financial gain for doing an unbelievable job. We're compensated the exact same if our idea generates 20 percent more business or even 70 percent. The only way we're not compensated is if we lose the client, so why risk it? Why innovate when mediocrity is so acceptable?

If you examine each and every monster idea we've explored in this book, we can see a significant risk/reward relationship. There was a risk in going that route, but the reward outweighed the risk. What could be gained was worth what could be lost. Fear of failure leads us to mediocrity as ideators and until failure is met with lessened consequence, we can't expect that to change.

Don't get me wrong, there are very serious consequences in the marketplace when an idea flops, but how many ideas that were on target emotionally, experientially, authentically, narratively, originally, and entertainmently (Okay, that one wasn't a word, I admit it. "Narratively" is suspect, too, but I was on a roll) have failed miserably in the marketplace? The answer is very few. No, fear of failure is just as much about failing to consider (or pitch) the monster idea as it is failing in the marketplace.

What keeps us from generating, expressing, developing, or pitching monster ideas? We're afraid they'll fail. We're afraid to be wrong. We're afraid to innovate because innovating is hard. It requires faith and trust and attention and devotion. Innovating takes considerably more energy and effort than not, so we choose to not be wrong and generate, express, develop, and pitch ideas that have little chance to fail but little chance to go monster, either. The agencies and entities that developed the ideas we explored in this book, at some point, decided they weren't afraid to fail. They created a culture that didn't just tolerate failure, they encouraged it. The reward for this culture are ideas that can, and have, gone monster.

We explored work from Nike's ad agency, Wieden + Kennedy, a few times through this book. They have created their fair share of monster ideas over the years, and they continue to innovate for a client that celebrates failure as part of the athletic process and so is part of their brand culture. It should be no surprise that W+K celebrates failure just as much. In 2006, a group of creatives from the Portland office bought out every clear pushpin on the West Coast (allegedly. I didn't personally attempt to procure a clear pushpin on the West Coast at the time so I have no hard evidence.) to create a mural that hung in the lobby. The mural had a simple message: Fail Harder. The message was derived from a piece of advice Dan Wieden gave to a creative director he once promoted. He told this new CD "You're no good to me until you've made at least three monumental mistakes." His advice was that we don't grow until we're willing to fall, fall, and fall hard.

Keeping with Wieden + Kennedy's failure theme, the W+K London office has a peculiar lobby installation of its own. In the foyer is a mannequin of a businessman walking, briefcase in hand. Something is clearly off about the pin-striped figure, though. His head is missing and in replacement is a common kitchen blender. Along with this, the briefcase is adorned with bright pink lettering affixed to the outside. It says "Walk in stupid every morning." Now while I subscribe to that theory based on the fact that I have no choice in the matter, the encouragement is far more purposeful on their end. W+K knows that we learn what we don't know and repeat what we know, so if we want to spend our creative energy learning and innovating, we have to be willing to try and fail.

There's a reason why I referred to this as the plus one in the "six plus one" formula for predicting monster potential in our marketing ideas—because fear isn't a quality, it's a reaction. Not all of the monster ideas we've explored in this book scared the creators of the idea, but they all contained elements that were scary. There was risk in each of them. What we learned is that we can't eliminate fear of failure but we can't let it drive our decisions, either. Monster ideas should scare us a little, they should make everyone at the table a little uneasy. That's part of how they turn monster. But that fear shouldn't keep us from generating, expressing, developing, or pitching an idea that is scary. As a matter of fact, fear may be the strongest indicator of an idea's potential that there is.

How many times have you generated an idea that initiated no fear whatsoever, there was nothing to be afraid of in the concept or execution of that idea, it was completely safe and harmless? Now, how many times has that idea gone monster for you? I'm betting very few. Fear is there for a reason, it's a warning mechanism that says "Danger, Will Robinson, danger!" (Disclosure: It may not call you 'Will Robinson' if your name is, say, Erica. It will probably call you by name. If it calls you by another name, there's a chance you may be crazy. You should see your doctor if that occurs. Don't call me. Seriously, don't call.) Fear is telling you the idea is dangerous. But what monster idea isn't dangerous? Monsters are dangerous, if they weren't, they'd be called ice cream cones. As marketers and advertisers, we should strive for a level of danger in our ideas. The only way they have a chance to go monstrous is if they also have a chance to shrivel and die violently. Anything in between has very little chance of growing monstrous at all.

Every one of us has the ability to generate monster ideas. We actually do it all the time. Sitting across from your friends at a bar table in a pub or laughing alongside your colleagues at lunch, we generate monster ideas, giggle at the possibilities and then toss them aside as the offspring of too many umbrella drinks or the punchline of too many sarcastic stories. These are often the genesis of monster ideas but we turn off the "what if" person we are for the "just" person we become the moment we generate ideas with consequences.

"Just" people are the folks at the table who aim to solve problems with the word "just." For example, "Why don't we just do this?" or "Let's just do that and be done with it." "Just" people solve problems in expected and inarguable ways by just solving it the same way they always have or just presenting the same idea someone else succeeded with. "Just" folks aren't interested in novelty or emotion or experience because the qualities require thought and planning and faith. An idea is an idea, after all. But I'm betting you're not reading this book because you're interested in just an idea. You're interested in monster ideas, the ones that explode when they hit the streets and take on a life of their own. Those types of ideas are never generated by "just" people. They're only generated by "what if" people.

My business partner, Mike Kelly, is prone to saying, "Wouldn't it be great if . . ." followed by some outrageous observation about food or music or travel. "Wouldn't it be great if . . . pizza was a diet food and you got increasingly thinner the more you ate it?" or "Wouldn't it be great if . . . there was a personal beer tap in front of every seat at the ballpark so you never had to get up to pour a frosty cold one at the game?" While these are clearly absurd desires (except the pizza one, that's legit), monster ideas come from people who aren't afraid to ask "what if?" If you were looking for the origin of every one of the ideas we've explored so far, you could generate a far more plausible "what if" question than a "just" solution.

What if we replayed unfinished high school sports games to determine the winner by bringing back all the participants of the game 15 years later and training them for the game?

What if you could walk up and down a staircase and each step acted like a piano key, playing a different note?

Why don't we just have an old guy who is super interesting and we tell the interesting stories of his life?

That last one just didn't sound right, did it? No, "what if" people are the folks that develop monster ideas because they're willing to set aside expectation and tradition and even their own comfort to develop something risky, something that scares them a little. It may not always turn monster in the way they hope, but you can be assured that their ability to suspend their fear of failure leads them to innovative examples. Right or wrong, executed perfectly or rough around the edges, the "what if" people have far greater successes in quality than the "just" people have in quantity.

A great example of a scary "what if" scenario happened in 2009 when ad shop Agency.com set aside an obvious and real fear to try something novel for client Mars on behalf of their brand, Skittles. In a bold move, the ad shop did away with the traditional home page for a candy brand like Skittles. No safe Flash games, no witty headlines twisting their familiar "Taste the Rainbow" tag, no signup boxes or flavor explanations. Instead, a direct and unfiltered Twitter feed of every post that included the word Skittles.

ARE YOU CRAZY!?

Agency.com just took the brand control away from the marketers and into the hands of the consumer. Unabated. Unprotected. Unfiltered. Anything and everything that was Tweeted with the word Skittles in it showed up on the home page of skittles.com, at least for a few seconds until it was replaced with the next post and so on. Everything. Every glowing praise of a particular flavor and every scathing hate bomb for the colored sugarpill. Everything, straight from the consumer. That's some cajones. Agency.com did what (almost) no one had dared to do, gave the brand to the consumer without edit. (I say "almost" because technically, branding firm Modernista! out of Boston, Massachusetts, did something similar with their own brand before the Skittles effort, choosing to have their Web site be a portal to how the Web sees their brand through search engines and social media.) Novelty aside, it was the first time in that bright of a spotlight that a brand chose to hand over the reins to the consumer without any editing and with such immediacy. We looked at GM in the authenticity chapter when they launched the Chevy Tahoe campaign where they allowed the consumer to make TV spots with their own text overlays for a contest, and while that is also turning the brand over to the consumer, the exchange here is considerably easier, more immediate, and more attainable as it only takes a Twitter post with the word Skittles in it to display on the home page of a major brand.

Agency.com felt that if they were going to use social media, and they wanted to have an authentic exchange with their target audience, then they needed to walk the walk. They were going to bank on the good will they'd earn through total transparency trumping anything negative that could be posted. They wanted the social universe to know that while they are a corporate brand, they are a brand that believes fully in the medium they choose to use and the audience to whom they choose to market. If they were going to say "be real," they had to prove "be real."

This is where the story gets interesting. The site was only up for two days when the social experiment took the turn everyone feared and pranksters started posting foul language, racial slurs, and other general profanities that Internet pranksters are prone to do when given the chance to be seen by such a large audience. They removed the Twitter feed and instead directed the home page to their Facebook fan page, a move that resulted in half a million fans by the end of the campaign. The amount of buzz the campaign has generated is inarguable, traditional media alone could never have charged so much so fast.

So was the frightening experiment a success or failure? Depends on your point of view. Some saw it as an unmitigated success, a buzz-generating machine that put a small candy in the limelight (or cherrylight, if you prefer) for a period of time that is impossible to create any other way. Some call it a complete and utter failure by handing over your brand message to consumers who are far more interested in themselves than your brand character. Whatever side of the fence you are on, there is no mistaking that generating, expressing, developing, or pitching that idea was scary. Was it a monster idea? Depends on who you ask but it's clear there would have been little chatter at all about Skittles had they run a traditional, safe campaign about the fruit-flavored candy.

So how do we alleviate this fear of failure? How do we produce ideas that have a higher chance at reaching monster status? It starts with first learning to accept failure as part of the creative process but more important, it starts with defining the types of failures we're looking to tolerate. There are dumb failures: failures that are a result of poor conceptual problem solving. Dumb failures are a repercussion of straying from the qualities we identified throughout the book, the characteristics of a monster idea. If we choose to be inauthentic or choose to be novel without developing relevance, we are setting ourselves up for a dumb failure. If we fail, it's because we missed the mark.

Smart failures, however, are ones that failed for other reasons, reasons that we couldn't control. They are on task, on track, and within the confines of the goal. They stay to the characteristics we've identified as monstrous idea qualities, but fell short for any number of reasons. Smart failures should be encouraged. Dumb failures should be taken out back and beaten with a mop handle (the failures, not the failure creators. Unless they deserved it.).

In a 2006 article titled "How Failure Breeds Success" for *Bloomberg Businessweek*, author Jena McGregor quotes Scott Anthony, the managing director at consulting firm Innosight, as he talked about smart failures: "Figuring out how to master this process of failing fast and failing cheap and fumbling toward success is probably the most important thing companies have to get good at." She follows up by saying, "'Getting good' at failure, however, doesn't mean creating anarchy out of organization. It means leaders—not just on a podium at the annual meeting, but in the trenches, every day—who create an environment safe for taking risks and who share stories of their own mistakes. It means bringing in outsiders unattached to a project's past. It means carving out time to reflect on failure, not just success."

To learn to reduce our fear of failure, we must be willing to first lower consequence and then be willing to fail smartly. Smart failures lead to insight, we learn from them. It's said we learn more from our failures than we do from our successes, but that's only true if our failures bring us usable insight, which means they have to be smart failures.

Do our ideas scare us? If we desire for them to be monster ideas, we should be actively seeking out something within that idea that does. We don't want that fear to debilitate us, but that fear is a sign that we are probably on the right track. Monster ideas are scary, anything novel or original usually is, but that fear should drive us to take a long, hard look at our idea, ensure that it's in line with the characteristics of a monster idea, then let it go. If it's a bad idea, we'll know as soon as we get that scathing Greek phone call, cursing in a language you can't understand but clearly hearing "cockroach" and "falafel." If it's a good idea, you just may have a monster on your hands. Master Chief would be proud.

The Aftermath

Acknowldgments

It's impossible to write anything of any size without a pile of people helping you out along the way (not a literal pile of people, that would be gross. Ish.). My pile of people includes my wife, Niqua, and daughter, Caitlyn, who peered through the office window on many nights wondering if I was done yet but gave me the time to finish anyway, my mom, who never needs to read or see anything I've ever worked on to say that I'm the best at it, ever (thanks, mom), and Erica Guthrie, who was my sounding board and informal idea editor throughout the writing of the book. Many of the features throughout the book, like the Xbox 360 Halo 3 example that we touch on in every chapter and the chapter Tear Sheets were her contributions, so you can thank her for all that is good here. It's an inevitability that I can one day offer to return the favor for her book. To my editor, Lauren, for her patience, enthusiasm, and understanding. To my production editor, Lauren (*no, the other one*), for her keen eye and ability to make my rambling coherent. To Von Glitschka for his incredible illustration talent with the monsters on the cover and for just being a great friend through the project. And last, to my business partner and friend, Mike Kelly, who helped form this philosophy with me and continually provides "wouldn't it be great if . . ." moments to test each one. He's an absolute monster idea maker and encourager extraordinaire. I'm lucky to have him and his eternal optimism in my life. If you know him, you already know what I mean.

Notes

Most of the examples cited throughout the book are pulled from experience and remembrance then backed up by various online and offline sources to fill in the often large gaps in my memory with relevant information. The following pages are a collection of those sources along with the agencies, firms, and individual creatives cited within the chapter. Not listed here are any examples or stories that I completely fabricated in an effort to impress you with my vast mental repository and wordsmithery.

Introduction

The campaign success referenced for the Nike "Whatever" campaign was pulled from a June 5, 2000, *Brandweek* article by Janis Mara:
http://findarticles.com/p/articles/mi_m0BDW/is_23_41/ai_62918979

The Ray Kroc story was pulled from an about.com post by Don Daszkowski on popular franchises:
http://franchises.about.com/od/mostpopularfranchises/a/ray-kroc-story.htm

The Apple/Motorola story was pulled from the Wiki article "History of the iPhone":
http://en.wikipedia.org/wiki/History_of_the_iPhone

The facts within the Subservient Chicken story can be backed up within the Wiki article "The Subservient Chicken":
http://en.wikipedia.org/wiki/The_Subservient_Chicken

The reference to the concept of sticky ideas comes from the book *Made to Stick* by Chip and Dan Heath; New York, Random House, 2007.

The recounting of the Microsoft Xbox 360 Halo 3 campaign by McCann Worldgroup SF and its subsequent success can be found in the Wiki article "Halo 3 Marketing": http://en.wikipedia.org/wiki/Marketing_for_Halo_3

"Does It Evoke An Emotional Response?"

The reference to the purchase value star comes from the book *Emotion Marketing: the Hallmark Way of Winning Customers for Life* by Scott Robinette and Claire Brand with Vicki Lenz; New York, McGraw-Hill, 2001.

The Nike "Just Do It" tag line story was pulled from a July 17, 2008, article by Brent Hunsberger titled "Nike celebrates 'Just Do It' 20th anniversary with new ad" in *The Oregonian*'s online counterpart, oregonlive.com:
http://blog.oregonlive.com/playbooksandprofits/2008/07/nike_celebrates_just_do_it_20t.html

The Center for Applied Research quote on the "Just Do It" slogan was pulled from an Ideamarketers.com article by Carry Anderson:
http://www.ideamarketers.com/?articleid=1407615

The DeBeer's "A Diamond Is Forever" *Advertising Age* ranking can be viewed here:
http://adage.com/century/slogans.html

The results of the Unbreakable Kiss campaign were documented on the Unbreakable Kiss campaign page of adsoftheworld.com:
http://adsoftheworld.com/media/dm/de_beers_diamonds_unbreakable_kiss

The *Mad Men* scene of Don Draper pitching the Eastman Kodak Carousel slide projector can be seen on YouTube here:
http://www.youtube.com/watch?v=suRDUFpsHus

The Gatorade "Replay" campaign details were pulled from a July 12, 2010, case study on Utalkmarketing.com:
http://www.utalkmarketing.com/Pages/Article.aspx?ArticleID=18303&Title=Gatorade_'Replay'_PR_campaign

The *Mission: Impossible 3* newspaper campaign story was pulled from a May 1, 2006, World Entertainment News article:
http://www.hollywood.com/news/Mission_Impossible_3_Stunt_Goes_Wrong/3497891

The *Aqua Teen Hunger Force* story came from multiple sources, including the Wiki article "2007 Boston Bomb Scare," the July 2007 CNN story "Two held after ad campaign triggers Boston bomb scare," and, January 2007 engadget.com article by Ryan Block titled "Aqua Teen Hunger Force viral ads cause Boston bomb scare":
http://en.wikipedia.org/wiki/2007_Boston_bomb_scare
http://articles.cnn.com/2007-01-31/us/boston.bombscare_1_bomb-scares-charlestown-district-court-peter-berdovsky?_s=PM:US
http://www.engadget.com/2007/01/31/aqua-teen-hunger-force-viral-ads-cause-boston-bomb-scare

The *Aqua Teen Hunger Force* bomb scare press conference that includes the response by the defendants can be seen on YouTube here:
http://www.youtube.com/watch?v=fJkTNJ7BM9I

The Tourism Queensland "The Best Job in the World" campaign facts and results can be viewed here: http://www.ourawardentry.com.au/bestjob/index.html

"Does It Create an Experience?"

The Apple Store history was pulled from the Wiki article "Apple Store":
http://en.wikipedia.org/wiki/Apple_Store

The quote about Apple's philosophy on customer service comes from the book *Punching In: One Man's Undercover Adventures on the Front Lines of America's Best-Known Companies* by Alex Frankel, New York, HarperCollins, 2007.

The story of the author who wrote her book at the Soho Apple Store was pulled from a June 28, 2006, FishbowlNY article titled "5'2" Homeless Model Writes Tragic-Cum-Triumphant Memoir at SoHo Apple Store":
http://www.mediabistro.com/fishbowlny/52-homeless-model-writes-tragic-cum-triumphant-memoir-at-soho-apple-store_b2528

The "Tryvertising" definition and source was pulled from an April 2005 trendwatching.com article titled "Tryvertising":
http://www.trendwatching.com/trends/tryvertising.htm

The L'Oréal digital mirrors campaign was sourced from a June 22, 2010, *Mediaweek* article by John Reynolds titled "L'Oréal weighs up 'digital mirror' kiosks":
http://www.mediaweek.co.uk/news/1011339/LOrEal-weighs-digital-mirror-kiosks

The Senseo Coffee Maker tram stop installation story was pulled from the trend-watching.com article titled "Tryvertising":
http://trendwatching.com/trends/TRYVERTISING.htm

The Ritz-Carlton/Mercedes-Benz story was pulled from a March 2005 Market Wire article titled "The Ritz-Carlton Introduces Mercedes-Benz CLS500 to 2005 Key to Luxury Package":
http://findarticles.com/p/articles/mi_pwwi/is_200503/ai_n13267746

The "Charmin Luxury Restroom" campaign details can be viewed here:
http://springwise.com/marketing_advertising/charmin_brand_space

The Yell.com "Results for Real Life" campaign details were pulled from an August 19, 2006, springwise.com article titled "Let Your Buses Do the Talking":
http://springwise.com/marketing_advertising/let_your_buses_do_the_walking

The term "Guerilla Marketing" originated from the book *Guerilla Marketing* by Jay Conrad Levinson, Boston, Houghton Mifflin Company, 1985.

The Salvation Army's "reverse graffiti" campaign details were pulled from a July 20, 2009, springwise.com article titled "Donated Guerilla Campaign Promotes Salvation Army": http://springwise.com/non-profit_social_cause/salvationarmy

The "Sea Tagging" campaign by media agency Curb was detailed in the April 22, 2009, springwise.com article "Latest Eco-Friendly Branding Tool: Sea Tagging":
http://springwise.com/eco_sustainability/seatagging

The reverse graffiti campaign for Tide detergent by Leo Burnett Frankfurt is detailed here: http://adsoftheworld.com/media/ambient/tide_longer?size=_original

The story of Halfway, Oregon, becoming half.com, Oregon, was pulled from the Wiki article "Halfway, Oregon": http://en.wikipedia.org/wiki/Halfway,_Oregon

The details and pictures of the "Domino's Delivery Points" campaign can be viewed here: http://springwise.com/marketing_advertising/dominosdoors

The Folgers Coffee manhole cover story is documented here:
http://www.coloribus.com/adsarchive/outdoor-ambient/folgers-coffee-steaming-manhole-8304005

The HP photo paper campaign makes almost no sense in text without seeing images of the installations in play, which can be viewed here:
http://cubeme.com/blog/2008/05/09/hp-advanced-photo-paper-by-publicis-malaysia

"Does It Entertain?"

The story of the "Luckytown" campaign was brilliantly detailed during an interview with then Barkley, Evergreen & Partners Senior Copywriter/now Callahan Creek Executive Creative Director Tug McTighe over a bucket of popcorn and a bevy of frothy mugs at The Brooksider in Kansas City, Missouri.

The quotes from Jon Bond of Kirshenbaum Bond & Partners came from a March 21, 2007, CNNMoney.com article by Paul R. La Monica titled "The Problem with TV Ads": http://money.cnn.com/2007/03/21/commentary/mediabiz/index.htm

The David Ogilvy quotes about entertainment were pulled from his book, *Ogilvy on Advertising*, New York, Random House, 1985.

The Jeff Fromm and John January quotes about the "Luckytown" campaign were pulled from a September 14, 1998, *Adweek* article by Aaron Baar titled "BE&P Puts 'Luckytown' On The Map": http://www.allbusiness.com/marketing-advertising/4180372-1.html

The Toyota Sienna campaign details, including quotes from Creative Director Erich Funke, were pulled from a brisk e-mail interview performed between April and July, 2010.

The "Swagger Wagon" rap video viewing numbers can be seen below the YouTube video.

The *Blair Witch Project* success numbers were pulled from the Wiki article titled "The Blair Witch Project": http://en.wikipedia.org/wiki/The_Blair_Witch_Project

The viewing numbers of the Old Spice spot from Wieden + Kennedy can be viewed below the YouTube video.

The average age of Internet users demographic information was pulled from an April 2010 eMarketer report by Lisa E. Philips: http://www2.emarketer.com/Reports/All/Emarketer_2000670.aspx

The campaign results for the "The Man Your Man Could Smell Like" campaign were pulled from an August 2010 Adweek blog post from Brian Morrissey titled "Old Spice's Agency Flexes Its Bulging Stats":
http://adweek.blogs.com/adfreak/2010/08/old-spices-agency-flexes-its-bulging-stats.html

If you're game, you can get all the Chuck Norris facts you're diaphragm can stomach: http://www.chucknorrisfacts.com

All of "The Most Interesting Man in the World" quotes can be found at: http://www.dosequis.com

The quotes by former Euro RSCG New York CCO Conway Williamson were pulled from an August 2009 *Maclean's* article titled "King of Beer Sales, Amigo":
http://www2.macleans.ca/2009/08/13/king-of-beer-sales-amigo

The details and results of BMW Films and *The Hire* were pulled from the Wiki article titled "The Hire": http://en.wikipedia.org/wiki/The_Hire

"Is It Novel?"

The UCL Institute of Cognitive Neuroscience study on novelty and memory and accompanying quotes by Dr. Emrah Düzel was documented in an August 2006 UCL article titled "Novelty Aids Learning":
http://www.physorg.com/news73834337.html

The Yankelovich Inc. quote regarding the number of advertising messages the average adult is exposed to appeared in a January 2007 *New York Times* article titled "Anywhere the eye can see, it is likely to see an ad":
http://www.yankelovich.com/index.php?option=com_content&task=view&id=163&Itemid=289&Itemid=1

The Leo Burnett quote about originality in advertising can be viewed many places online along with other brilliant Burnett quotes including:
http://www.brandingstrategyinsider.com/2010/10/the-advertising-wisdom-of-leo-burnett.html

The New Mexico urinal cake campaign was pulled from a February 2007 CBSNews article titled "Say Again? Talking Urinal Cakes Introduced":
http://www.cbsnews.com/stories/2007/02/15/national/main2482778.shtml

The quote from Terry Marks appears in the Rule29/tmarksdesign collaborative 5th Year Anniversary self promo book "Rules 1–28."

CP+B's "Whopper Sacrifice" story was pulled from a January 2009 *Adweek* article titled "Whopper Sacrifice Ends" and an April 2009 CNET News article titled "The dark secrets of Whopper Sacrifice":
http://www.adweek.com/aw/content_display/news/digital/
e3i0b84325122066ed91cf3de61d0656f6e
http://news.cnet.com/8301-13577_3-10211898-36.html

The IKEA Facebook campaign was documented in the CNET News November 2009 article titled "IKEA's brilliant Facebook campaign":
http://news.cnet.com/8301-1023_3-10404937-93.html

The Nokia Silence Booths can be viewed here:
http://www.guerrilla-innovation.com/archives/2006/08/000515.php

The Dommelsch beer pop-up concert story was pulled from a March 2006 trenwatching.com article titled "Being Spaces & Brand Spaces":
http://www.trendwatching.com/trends/brand-spaces.htm

The Toys 'R' Us inflatable globe story will make much more sense when you see the picture here: http://adsoftheworld.com/media/ambient/toysrus_inflatable_globe?size=_original

The HBO *The Sopranos* guerilla campaign is illuminated with images of the taxi cabs here: http://blog.guerrillacomm.com/2007/04/guerrilla-marketing-sopranos.html

Pics of the Panasonic Lumix ZX1 guerilla campaign and a campaign explanation can be found here: http://www.adverblog.com/archives/004164.htm

The story of Alec Brownstein and his Google Job Experiment can be viewed at his YouTube site: http://www.youtube.com/watch?v=7FRwCs99DWg

The VW "Fun Theory" story was pulled straight from the source:
http://www.thefuntheory.com

The Paul Rand quote about originality came from Paul Rand himself in this video:
http://www.logodesignlove.com/paul-rand-video

"Is It Authentic?"

The ill-fated McDonald's campaign described can be found ad nauseam throughout the Web, but a few instances are provided here:

http://www.adrants.com/2005/01/mcdonalds-wants-people-to-fornicate.php
http://www.bloggingstocks.com/2008/09/07/ads-gone-bad-what-did-mcdonalds-think-id-hit-that-meant-any

The 2005 Sony PSP graffiti brushback was detailed in a December 2005 *Wired* article titled "Sony Draws Ire With PSP Graffiti":

http://www.wired.com/culture/lifestyle/news/2005/12/69741

The Target/Walmart Facebook campaigns, including accompanying quotes by the major players in the campaigns, were detailed in an October 2007 *Adweek* article by Joan Voight titled "Social Marketing Do's And Don'ts" and in consecutive posts on social-media-optimization.com:

http://www.adweek.com/aw/esearch/article_display.jsp?vnu_content_id=1003654896
http://social-media-optimization.com/2007/10/a-successful-facebook-marketing-campaign
http://social-media-optimization.com/2007/10/a-failed-facebook-marketing-campaign

Details and facts from the Sony PSP/Zipatoni story have been documented in a variety of places, a few are listed below:

http://en.wikipedia.org/wiki/Zipatoni
http://www.wired.com/gamelife/2006/12/sonys_failed_ps
http://adage.com/smallagency/post?article_id=113945

The Chevy Tahoe user-generated content campaign was documented in an April 2006 *New York Times* article by Julie Bosman titled "Chevy Tries a Write-Your-Own-Ad Approach, and the Potshots Fly":

http://www.nytimes.com/2006/04/04/business/media/04adco.html

The details regarding stealth marketing can be found in an April 2010 New York Daily News article by staff writer Jacob E. Osterhout titled "Stealth marketing: When you're being pitched and you don't even know it!":

http://www.nydailynews.com/lifestyle/2010/04/19/2010-04-19_stealth_marketing_when_youre_being_pitched_and_you_dont_even_know_it.html

"Does It Tell a Story?"

The steamboat *Arabia* facts can be found at: http://www.1856.com

The steamboat *Arabia* fictions can be found in my head somewhere, but the facts regarding John Calvin McCoy can be found on the Wiki entry titled "John Calvin McCoy": http://en.wikipedia.org/wiki/John_Calvin_McCoy

The Owen Flanagan quote is documented all over the Interweb, like here: http://www.museumstuff.com/learn/topics/narrative

The reference to Malcolm Gladwell is referring to his book, *The Tipping Point: How Little Things Can Make a Big Difference*; Boston, Little, Brown & Company, 2000.

The quote regarding the power of story comes from the book *Made to Stick* by Chip and Dan Heath; New York, Random House, 2007.

The story of Apple's "1984" spot was pulled from the Wiki entry titled "1984 (commercial)": http://en.wikipedia.org/wiki/1984_(television_commercial)

The list of TV spots referenced as stories can be seen on Youtube:
Jell-O: http://www.youtube.com/watch?v=mjrtsIY4WqQ
Budweiser Frogs: http://www.youtube.com/watch?v=f3mXaATLeRM
Joe Isuzu: http://www.youtube.com/watch?v=A0bJ5iB_DqQ
Brain on Drugs: http://www.youtube.com/watch?v=nl5gBJGnaXs
Energizer Bunny: http://www.youtube.com/watch?v=QxafIhYFOr0
Where's the Beef?: http://www.youtube.com/watch?v=Ug75diEyiA0
Tastes Great, Less Filling: http://www.youtube.com/watch?v=omB-HVs6sRw
Life cereal: http://www.youtube.com/watch?v=vYEXzx-TINc

The details of HBO's "The Cube" installation was pulled from a September 2009 PSFK article titled "4-Way Narrative: HBO's Video Cube Installation": http://www.psfk.com/2009/09/4-way-narrative-hbos-video-cube-installation.html

The "Art of the Heist" details are documented on both the Wiki entry titled "The Art of the Heist" and the McKinney corporate agency Web site:
http://en.wikipedia.org/wiki/The_Art_of_the_Heist
http://mckinney.com/work/clients/audi/art-of-the-h3ist

Details of Steven Spielberg's *Artificial Intelligence: AI* film alternate reality game, The Beast, can be found on the Wiki entry titled "The Beast (game)" and on 42 Entertainment's corporate agency website:

http://en.wikipedia.org/wiki/The_Beast_(game)
http://www.42entertainment.com/beast.html

The Volvo *Pirates of the Caribbean* ARG is documented in a number of places:

http://www.motortrend.com/auto_news/112_news060629_pirates_of_the_caribbean_volvo_xc90_hunt/index.html
http://promomagazine.com/contests/volvo_2007_pirates_treasure_hunt_032007

The quote from Jim Loehr is from his book, *The Power of Story: Change Your Story, Change Your Destiny in Business and in Life*, New York, Free Press, 2007.

Chris King's quote is from her blog, *Storytelling Power*:

http://www.creativekeys.net/StorytellingPower/article1004.html

"Does It Scare You?"

You can watch Mola Ram rip the heart out of the human sacrifice in *Indiana Jones and the Temple of Doom* here:

http://www.youtube.com/watch?v=owZPspxJ4jw

The story of Wieden + Kennedy's "Fail Harder" mural can be found here:

http://www.swiss-miss.com/2009/10/fail-harder.html

You can see a pic of Wieden + Kennedy's London office foyer here:

http://wklondon.typepad.com/welcome_to_optimism/2010/06/wiedens-stupid-approach-endorsed-by-harvard-business-review.html

The Agency.com/Skittles story was pulled from a March 2009 *Wall Street Journal* article by Emily Steel titled "Skittles Cozies Up to Social Media" while the aftermath of the campaign stunt was pulled from mediabistro.com:

http://online.wsj.com/article/SB123604377921415283.html
http://www.mediabistro.com/prnewser/skittles-re-skins-website-with-twitter-search-page-world-still-revolves-around-sun_b1497?c=rss

The Scott Anthony quote came from a 2006 *Bloomberg Businessweek* article by Jena McGregor titled "How Failure Breeds Success":

http://www.businessweek.com/innovate/content/jul2006/id20060702_006446.htm

Index

A

A Diamond is Forever, 36
adidas, 73
Advertising Age magazine, 36
Affair, The, 170
Agency.com, 191
AKQA, 68, 117, 136, 137
Amazon, 64
Anthony, Scott, 194
Apple, 19, 20, 54, 56, 57, 58, 59, 60, 61, 164
Apple Store, 54
Aqua Teen Hunger Force, 45, 46
Arabia, 154, 155, 156, 158
ARG; Alternate Reality Gaming, 77, 78, 170, 171, 172, 173, 177
Art of the Heist, the, 171
Audi, 171, 172
audience authenticity, 131, 140, 149

B

Barkley Evergreen & Partners, 85, 86
BBDO, 22, 169
BBH/London, 168
Beast, The, 172
Best Job in the World, The, 47
Blair Witch Project, 91
Bloomberg Businessweek, 194
BMW, 97, 98, 168
Bond, Jon, 85, 88
brand authenticity, 131, 149
Brand, Claire, 33
brand evangelism, 144
brand exchange, 67, 73, 95, 116, 133, 143
brand experience, 56, 57, 62, 76, 79, 115, 166, 170, 181
Brownstein, Alec, 118
Burger King, 91, 113
Burnett, Leo, 72, 111, 112

C

D

M

N

O

P

R

V

value, 6, 31, 32, 39, 60, 85, 86, 89, 100, 113, 116, 117, 133
Vertical Football, 73
viral, 19, 70, 90, 91, 92, 93, 94, 115, 140, 141, 143
Virgin, 165, 166
Volkswagen, 120, 131
Volvo, 127, 129, 130, 172, 173
Voyeur, 22

W

Walk in stupid every morning, 188
Walmart, 30, 136, 138, 139
weasels, 131
Wieden + Kennedy; W+K, 34, 92, 93, 95, 166, 188, 189
Wieden, Dan, 34
"what if," 191
Whopper Sacrifice, 113, 114
Williamson, Conway, 96

X

Xbox 360 Halo 3, 23, 49, 77, 78, 100, 122, 148, 174

Y

Yell.com, 68

Z

Zipatoni, 140